Moving
Up
and
Out

Moving
Up
and
Out

Poverty, Education,
and the Single Parent Family

Lori Holyfield

Foreword by
Hillary Rodham Clinton

Temple University Press
PHILADELPHIA

Temple University Press, Philadelphia 19122
Copyright © 2002 by Temple University, except
  Foreword copyright © 2002 by Hillary Rodham Clinton
All rights reserved
Published 2002
Printed in the United States of America

☉ The paper used in this publication meets the requirements of
the American National Standard for Information Sciences—Permanence
of Paper for Printed Library Materials, ANSI Z39.48-1984

Library of Congress Cataloging-in-Publication Data

Holyfield, Lori, 1960–
  Moving up and out: poverty, education, and the single parent family /
Lori Holyfield; foreword by Hillary Rodham Clinton.
    p.   cm.
  Includes bibliographical references and index.
  ISBN 1-56639-914-9 (cloth : alk. paper) — ISBN 1-56639-915-7 (pbk. : alk.
paper)
    1. Poor women—Arkansas.   2. Single mothers—Arkansas.   3. Women
heads of households—Arkansas.   4. Single mothers—Education—Social
aspects—Arkansas.   5. Women heads of households—Education—Social
aspects—Arkansas.   6. Single mothers—Scholarships, fellowships, etc.—
Arkansas.   7. Women heads of households—Scholarships, fellowships, etc.—
Arkansas.   8. Arkansas Single Parent Scholarship Fund.   9. Social mobility—
Arkansas.   10. Poverty—Arkansas.   1. Title.

HV1446.A8 H65 2002
362.83'92'09767—dc21

2001034717

In Memory of Diane Blair

Contents

Foreword

When Ralph Nesson first approached me about becoming the founding Board President of the Arkansas Single Parent Scholarship Program, I had to think hard about the wisdom of taking on any additional responsibilities. At the time, in 1989, I was First Lady of Arkansas, had a busy private law practice, was rearing a young child, and already had extensive community commitments. However, the more I thought about the daily desperation facing so many young parents, the more convinced I became of the enormous potential this program had for dealing with that desperation in a practical, productive, and lasting way. And my dear friend, Professor Diane Blair, convinced me we had to try to expand the program's reach and success.

Eleven years later, now that over six thousand scholarships have been awarded through this program to single parents whose lives have been transformed permanently for the better, I am very grateful I was given an opportunity to help bring this program to life. I hope this book will inform and inspire many others, who will then replicate the program in their own states and communities.

The goal of the Single Parent Scholarship Fund is to assist poor single parents to complete the higher education which is indispensable for skilled employment and family economic security in today's world. Even the most ambitious and determined of single parents often finds herself or himself struggling against an array of discouraging factors:

the high cost of tuition and books; the scarcity and expense of good day care; the absence of extended family or friends to provide backup day care and emotional support; the lack of reliable transportation; the lack of information about available scholarships and other assistance. No wonder so many become discouraged, and the downhill spiral begins.

The Single Parent Scholarship Program begins by directing recipients toward every form of tuition and scholarship assistance available for post-secondary education. It provides guidance toward all public and private assistance, everything from housing to health care, for which recipients and their children may be eligible. Recipients are offered mentoring by knowledgeable and responsible adults in their communities. And then the scholarship itself is awarded, usually $500 per semester for those who are making good progress toward graduation. That amount may seem negligible to some, but in fact it often provides the indispensable margin between success and failure.

The uses of that money are as varied as the lives of the individuals involved—everything from child care to car repairs, school shoes to utility bills. One woman memorably recounted for me how she had been unable, prior to the Single Parent Scholarship, to take certain courses necessary for her degree because of the laboratory fees involved and the cost of a lab coat, essential expenses simply not covered by her tuition assistance. Another woman was able to purchase automobile insurance, another bought two new tires for her car, without which these women were literally immobilized. It is the flexibility in the use of the money that makes it so valuable to scholarship recipients, not only for its monetary worth but for its symbolic meaning. Many scholarship recipients tell us that simply knowing that others had enough confidence in them to invest in their lives and trust their judgment was a powerful and uplifting agent for change.

Scholarship recipients have told me that often the biggest beneficiaries of the scholarship are their children, who, watching their moms taking their schooling so seriously, become much better students themselves. One woman related that she was on the verge of dropping out of college, worried that the sacrifices she was asking of her children were just too weighty; but her son's schoolteacher told her, "Don't you dare drop out. Not a day goes by that your son doesn't brag to his classmates that his Mom's going to be an engineer."

The stories of degrees earned, good jobs obtained, children's lives immeasurably improved are an endless source of gratification to the volunteers and contributors who have brought this program to maturity all across Arkansas. However, the evidence of this program's success is much more than anecdotal. At this writing, forty-eight counties are represented by Arkansas Single Parent Scholarship Fund affiliates; and an extensive follow-up survey conducted in 1997 indicated that 69 percent of graduates were employed at higher than poverty-level wages.

And what better evidence of this program's effectiveness could there be than the fact that the author of this volume, Lori Holyfield, herself one of the program's first scholarship recipients, used the funds to earn a degree from the University of Arkansas, went on to secure a Ph.D., and is now a member of the University of Arkansas faculty. I know Lori shares my hopes that the information provided in her book will be used by many others, to establish Single Parent Scholarship Funds in their own communities.

There is no reason that this wonderful idea can't work in places beyond Arkansas. Local businesses, foundations, churches, civic organizations, and private citizens can join together to form their own scholarship funds and their own committees, designed to help single parents in their communities lift themselves and their families out of poverty on a permanent basis. The investment is minimal. But the rewards for the recipient, their communities, and all those who become involved, are rich indeed.

Hillary Rodham Clinton

Preface

While teaching introductory sociology to students from a variety of backgrounds, I have become convinced that popular opinion greatly inflates the power of the individual. This celebration of the American notion of "rags to riches" comes to us at a high cost. As we focus on the ideal of individualism, we often forget that community is essential to these efforts. Community-sponsored programs that foster education, health, and well-being are now necessary to compensate for widespread cuts in federal programs such as welfare. Moreover, we often gasp at the mere suggestion that community might be *obligated* to aid in this process as more and more of America's children slip through the safety net and into poverty.

Perhaps it seems odd that one would write a book about the beneficiaries of a program that provides just a few hundred dollars in scholarship support. After all, the soaring costs of education will require a much larger financial base than what the Arkansas Single Parent Scholarship Fund (ASPSF) can offer. Indeed, when I first began this project some of my colleagues were skeptical. They asked, "How can a few hundred dollars make such a big difference?" My response was typically, "Because this particular scholarship is rich in symbolism." For most poor single mothers, just the opportunity to obtain a post-secondary education is an empowering first step in their journey toward independence. "Imagine being someone for whom opportunities have been blocked all your life," I would tell them, "and an organization from your *own* community—*not* the federal government, *not* the state, *not* some nameless corporation—but people from your own community have stepped up to say, 'We believe in you.'" I would add, "Remember it's a scholarship, not a hand-out." For many scholarship recipients, myself included, it was as if members of our community had managed to clear for us a small path to self-sufficiency. We had to walk those paths on our own, no doubt, but we did it with their financial and moral support.

My intention in writing this book is twofold. First, I want to shed light on the real lives of single parent families. Second, I hope to encourage readers to consider establishing a Single Parent Scholarship Fund in their own community.

It is also my hope that this book will not become one of those dusty relics that we place high on our bookshelves and only take down occasionally to remind ourselves of the numbing statistics surrounding poverty in the United States. The stories I am about to share with you belong to single mothers throughout Arkansas. They echo the stories of single parents across this country: single moms who struggle, hope, and dream of self-sufficiency.

Of the approximately 14 million single parent households in the United States, about two million are currently single father headed families. I interviewed three single fathers in the early stages of research and found that their struggles were in some ways similar to those of women. However, while the Scholarship is made available to both single moms and dads, over 99 percent of the beneficiaries are women. Because of the small number of fathers available for the study and the unique problems single mothers face, for the purpose of this book I chose to focus specifically upon the women, their families, and their struggles.

The women you will meet in this book are just a few of the millions of single parents who understand that raising children in the face of poverty is a huge task, no matter the individual circumstances. The difference, however, is that for many of the women in this book, the likelihood of experiencing a life free of welfare dependency has been greatly enhanced by a little-known program titled the Arkansas Single Parent Scholarship Fund.

The research that led to the writing of this book began in the spring of 1999. My meetings with the women who participated in this project were not by chance; I knew before I met them that their stories were also my own. As both a sociologist interested in poverty and an early beneficiary of the Scholarship, I wanted to know if obtaining an education was as much a life-changing event for others as it was for me.

In May of 1999 I received a small grant to study the histories of women who had participated in the Scholarship Fund and to examine what barriers they faced in obtaining their education. The funding allowed me to hire two graduate students for summer research and to travel throughout Arkansas and conduct in-depth interviews with former Scholarship recipients.

Various county affiliates of the Scholarship Fund provided the names of both current and former recipients. The research took place in two phases: phase one included interviews with those who had graduated from a postsecondary institution and were now employed, and phase two included those who dropped out of school and were no longer receiving the scholarship. The second phase was completed in the fall of 2000.

With the aid of graduate students, fifty-three individuals were interviewed for the project. Each was given a pseudonym. Some interviews were conducted in the homes of former recipients, some in restaurants, and some took place in work settings. Without exception, each woman was willing to share her experiences, both good and bad. Forty-one single mothers were asked to describe their journeys and to identify the most important barriers faced by single parents today. Many of their stories will be presented throughout the book. We asked them about being poor and of the struggles they faced. We asked about their dreams for the future and how obtaining an education has changed those dreams over time. We asked about their expectations for their children and what they believe the future now holds.

Many of the women are now finished with their educations and are gainfully employed at wages well above poverty level. What do they identify as the most important ingredients for success? Were the benefits worth the struggle? Do they look back on their experiences in similar or different ways, and what advice would they give to other single parents?

Even though the graduation rate is remarkable for those who receive the scholarships (an average of 70 percent throughout fifty-five participating counties), a significant number of single parents do drop out of school. I spoke to twelve of them to better understand the barriers they encountered. I wanted to hear their stories and learn whether their situations were similar to or different from those who graduated. What were some of the conditions they faced while attending school and how did those affect their choices? Were there ways that nonprofit organizations such as ASPSF could help prevent the conditions that led to dropping out?

The first five chapters comprise an attempt to weave together the statistical data with the actual lived experiences of single mothers and their children. The Introduction explains something of my own family's journey out of poverty and the role of the Arkansas Single Parent Scholarship Fund in that journey. Chapter 1 begins with just a few of the "before" and "after" narratives of women who have benefited from obtaining their education. Chapter 1 also addresses the issue of poverty, providing a broader context for the issue of welfare and its relationship to the single parent family.

In these five chapters, the voices of the women who participated in this project are interwoven to demonstrate how policies and moral rhetoric impact their lives and the lives of their children. Chapters 1 and 2 both document the barriers single parents face. Chapter 2 outlines welfare reform and policy. It discusses the implications for single parent families attempting to gain their education under current law. Chapter 3 examines the myths and images single mothers confront and the social stigma they have experienced in their sometimes long journey out of poverty.

Chapter 4 addresses education and mobility. In this chapter, I draw upon sociological analysis of our "credentialized" society and review the impact education has upon social mobility as well as its limitations. Also included is a discussion of the implications education has for the children of single parent families. Chapter 5 draws upon the voices of single mothers again, who explain the obstacles that led them to drop out or the benefits education has brought them.

Combined, Chapters 6 and 7 provide a framework that may be used by readers from other states as they attempt to influence policy and establish similar programs. Chapter 6 documents the philosophy and organizational structure behind the Arkansas Single Parent Scholarship Fund, and highlights the power of giving and the importance it holds for donors and volunteers as well. It is intended to provide readers with suggestions for implementing a grassroots scholarship fund and strategies for building an advisory board, raising donations, and building an endowment. Chapter 7 discusses policy suggestions that could help reduce poverty among single parent families and facilitate their greater participation in post-secondary education. It returns to the specific reasons single parent scholarships are so needed, not just in Arkansas but throughout the country. Appendix A provides the constitution and bylaws of the Arkansas Single Parent Scholarship Fund, and Appendix B contains a list of nonprofit resources for those readers interested in establishing a scholarship or similar program.

Acknowledgments

The seed for this book was planted years ago. In the mid-1980s, Ralph Nesson and the board of the Single Parent Scholarship Fund in Washington County, Arkansas, made an impression upon me that I would not realize for years to come. They simply cared about my future. They encouraged me to aim high, and to change the odds for myself and my daughter. They instilled in me a desire to give something back to a community that has given so much to so many single parent families.

I wish to thank the Jones Family–Community Institute and the Arkansas Community Foundation for generous grants that allowed me to collect the interviews and data that would lead to this book. Without their initial support, I could not have pursued this project.

The Arkansas Single Parent Scholarship Fund provided resources that enabled me to secure release time from teaching in order to focus on writing this book. One hundred percent of the proceeds from this book will be returned to the Arkansas Single Parent Scholarship Fund. I also wish to thank James Allred for his generous private contribution, which helped offset those costs to the fund. Finally, I thank the Walton Family Foundation for its charitable support in underwriting the publication of this book. Together, these benefactors made this project a reality.

Three excellent graduate assistants aided in the interviewing and transcription process. Without the help of

Robert Mortenson, Lorna Watkins, and Madelyn Phillips, I would still be transcribing my interviews today. Traci Yates, my graduate assistant, and Sarah House, an undergraduate work-study student, were of tremendous help in conducting library research for the project. The photograph for the cover of the book was generously donated by Don House of House Photoworks.

I consider myself to be extremely lucky to have family and friends who have collectively supported me throughout this endeavor. My daughter has given me the incentive to keep writing "so that others can know how college changes lives." My husband continues to amaze me with love, humor, and constant support.

Last, but certainly not least, I want to express sincere gratitude to the single parents throughout Arkansas who gave up precious time to share their personal journeys. Without their kindness, this book would not have been possible. They are strong and resilient women who renewed my faith in community and the power of the human spirit.

Moving
Up
and
Out

Introduction

Megan was five when she and I moved to our small rent-supported house on Pettigrew Street. Her father and I had divorced when she was two, and contact between them was infrequent until she reached the age of twelve and he reached sobriety. Technically it would be incorrect to say we lived on the "other side" of the tracks, but we were one block from them—close enough by most standards. Our house was on the corner of a dead-end street that served as the entrance to a local factory. It was not exactly a quiet neighborhood. The workers arrived a little before 6:00 A.M. and apparently dislodged their mufflers just before turning onto our street, as if to say, "We're here, we're loud, get used to it!" We never did.

It was a small frame house with two tiny bedrooms. The house had a stench to it when we moved in, a mixture of Pine-Sol and roach spray, that we were never able to get rid of. Its windows were perpetually fogged from the gases released between the double panes. It felt like Christmas year-round until a friend explained that it meant the insulation was no longer working. Megan and I made cut-out snowflakes and pasted them to the windows anyway.

The house did have its amusing features. A furnace, the type that stretches from the floor to the ceiling, was located in the living room on the wall between our bedrooms. Both Megan and I were sure it was haunted. When the thermostat kicked in, flames would burst out several inches

1

from the bottom. Sometimes we tip-toed past it just to see if we might outsmart the fiery demon. It was, after all, our first home since the divorce that did not have wood heat and did not require stoking in the middle of the night. Although we did not own a lawn mower, we at least had a small patch of lawn, which was a far cry better than the alternative, a housing authority apartment.

Megan's birthday fell in October, making her too young to enroll in first grade that year. But she was too old to attend another year of Head Start, so I enrolled her in a private nursery school a few blocks away from our home and paid almost one-third of my paycheck to keep her there. There may have been assistance for child care, but I was a full-time worker and did not receive AFDC (Aid to Families with Dependent Children). If I was eligible for assistance, I never knew it. Besides, I felt humiliated enough every time I paid the rent, or bought groceries with the small allotment of food stamps we received. I dreaded the disapproving glances at the check-out counter, and imagined people watching to see if I really drove a Cadillac. I paid the child care expenses myself, and we held on as best we could.

I tried several things to keep Megan and myself afloat after the divorce. I waited tables, stocked produce, worked the graveyard shift in a factory, played in an R&B band, and washed windows on weekends. Still, by 1982 I had run out of options and decided to try construction work. This was, after all, "man's" work and was sure to pay better than what I had been earning. And with only a ninth-grade education, I knew this was probably the best I could do. I worked on bridges, tied steel, and finished concrete, but remained a "laborer" (a nicer term for the lowest-paid worker).

I wanted more for Megan and myself but couldn't get there, not without an education. And no matter how hard I was willing to work, Megan and I barely remained afloat. We never had a telephone; that would have been a luxury. I paid the bills in a sporadic fashion, the light bill one month, the gas and water the next. I remember watching an episode of the sit-com *Roseanne* a few years ago. Roseanne was explaining to her husband how she had learned to keep the utilities on by sending the gas company the check for the light bill, and the light company the water bill, and so on. I remember joking, "I thought I was the only one who did that!" But there was little humor to our real-life situation. For Megan and I, poverty and everything that came with it seemed to clench its fist and pound us with no mercy. Sometimes we skimmed the surface; sometimes we bobbed up and down. All too often we came up gasping for air just before we were sucked under again. It was as if all the exits out of poverty were blocked—and indeed they were, but not for the reasons I thought.

Opportunities *were* being blocked, but I had never studied sociology and did not know that there is a direct correlation between education and poverty. I did not realize that as many as 24 percent of those without at least a high school diploma live in poverty. I was not aware that with a college education, the chances of living in poverty dropped dramatically, to just 2 percent. I just knew that I was unlucky! I did not realize that, without an education, this was truly as good as it would ever be. All I knew was that I was divorced, willing to work and struggle for my family, and it simply was not enough. It was the little things that kept us down: a toothache, the flu, the measles, a day missed from work, a car that failed to start. Preventive health care and wellness programs were not in my vocabulary. As with 44 million other Americans, health insurance for us was only a dream.

High school diplomas were certainly valued in my family, but neither of my parents finished high school. My older sister and brother had, however, and they both encouraged me to take the GED (high school equivalency) examination in the winter of 1983. I followed their advice and passed the exam. Then, after months of heavy prodding on their part, I enrolled at the University of Arkansas, terrified of what lay ahead.

College was another world indeed, and my romantic image of it left me ill prepared for what I would encounter. Studying did not come easy for me. In fact, much of my first year can best be described as an "adjustment period." Megan was doing well in the first grade and I was trying to convince myself that I really could be a student. As for so many single parent students, study time was relegated to a few hours in the library between classes and late in the evening after Megan was asleep. Although my confidence was starting to build, I lived in constant fear that my professors would find me out and realize I was a fraud who lacked all the necessary capital for this investment. Sooner or later someone would show me the door.

I was entering my second semester when I met Ralph Nesson, the director of the Single Parent Scholarship Fund. He was working in a dilapidated building that housed the Economic Opportunity Agency (EOA) of Washington County, where I had come more than once to seek help with utility bills. I don't remember how I found out about the Scholarship Fund, but I remember my meeting with Ralph very well. Earlier encounters with service agencies, especially the Department of Human Services, child-support enforcement, and the housing authority, had made me more than a little skeptical about the interview. I fully expected the all-too-familiar humiliation of having to prove my eligibility for the "entitlement" about to be bestowed upon me. But I resolved to go through the process if it would help me stay in school another semester.

The meeting did not happen as I had expected. Ralph greeted me with a warm smile, invited me into his office, and we sat down to discuss the scholarship application. Ralph asked me about my daughter and how I was doing. He asked me about college and my experiences there. I answered politely, sure the bottom would drop out at any moment. I had come to distrust such situations; they always seemed more like an interrogation than a conversation, and I always left feeling worse about myself than when I came in. But this was different. Ralph told me how proud he was that I took the chance of returning to school and said that he knew it was a risk. He said he understood it was difficult to get by financially, even on the student loans and Pell grant, and he asked if I knew about the Supplemental Educational Opportunity Grant and other forms of aid that might help. Apologetically, Ralph explained that while the fund did not have a lot of money to give, he could offer a $300 scholarship and that maybe I could use it to help with child care, or gas, or to fix my car, just whatever I felt was needed. I thought to myself, What, no need for deference? No ritual of humiliation? I didn't have to promise to spend the funds for this or that purpose? No receipts to prove how I spent the money? Not this time. He trusted me to know best.

I received the scholarship throughout the remainder of my undergraduate studies, using the money for everything from child care and transportation to books and materials.

I remember that I looked forward to the interviews with the scholarship board each semester because it offered me an opportunity to share with them the positive changes in my life. I gained more confidence with each successful semester. Looking back today, I believe those encounters with members of my own community made the difference.

My story could have been the story of thousands of women who have struggled to edge their way out of poverty. The fact that my story ends happily, however, is in large part due to the generosity of the Scholarship Fund and the various other forms of financial aid I received. But the empowerment I experienced in that initial meeting with Ralph Nesson was also remarkable. It must be difficult to understand the symbolic importance of an experience such as this unless one's self-esteem has truly hit bottom. I remember thinking, "A scholarship for me? Does he really think I can do this?" As it turns out, he did. Indeed, so did the board members, the many volunteers, and the donors to the Scholarship Fund. Fourteen years later, in a meeting with state legislators, I listened as Ralph described the program, which now assists single parents statewide and has an endowment of over $1 million, as a "barn raising" experience, one that allows the community to give to others. He was right.

The Single Parent Scholarship Fund began as a small grassroots effort in 1984. The mission was a simple one, as Ralph recalls: "We wanted to help single mothers get the education that would provide them with rewarding jobs, so they wouldn't need our help anymore and instead be able to give back to the community in productive ways."

The fund was the brainchild of a small group of people in northwest Arkansas. Ralph, then director of EOA, and Marjorie Marugg-Wolfe, the director of adult education and the displaced-homemakers program at a local technical school, had often discussed the unmet needs of their low-income clients and the barriers many of them faced to completing their education. Ralph recalls that during one of their many conversations on this topic, Marjorie interjected, "If you really want to do something to help lower-income people go to school, think about the women with children." Ralph agreed: Women with children were in many ways the ones who most needed opportunities to continue their educations but also had the fewest resources to do so.

Women would often come into the vocational-technical school where Marjorie worked and look up courses they might take, then walk right back out the door when they saw the costs. Among all the barriers they faced, the financial costs ranked high. Consequently, Ralph and Marjorie wanted to find a way to provide financial incentives to single parents without all the red tape and bureaucratic entanglements of other programs. A scholarship would do both! And so the Single Parent Scholarship Fund was born. Neither Ralph nor Marjorie could have predicted that sixteen years later the fund would operate statewide and would have provided over six thousand Arkansans with scholarship assistance. I will return to the Arkansas Single Parent Scholarship Fund in Chapter 6 to say more about its philosophy and successes.

1 It Ain't That Simple

We can talk about poverty, the millions of working poor and the viability of the welfare system, but only by understanding how these abstract notions play out in the lives of hardworking Americans can we cut through the numbing statistics and conflicting arguments.
—Schwarz and Volgy 1992

Imagine it is 3:00 A.M. on the "heart/liver" line in a poultry-processing plant. Patricia stands at attention in front of the stainless steel trough. Ice cold water stings even through the latex gloves. The scissors are sharp enough to sever a finger in a careless moment. Hanging by their feet, headless chickens approach her on the line. She quickly yanks the heart and liver, snips the soft tissue, and the next bird appears before another breath is taken.

After seven years on the graveyard shift, Patricia hardly notices the coppery scent of blood mixed with the more subtle smell of burnt beaks and feathers. Nor does she acknowledge the caustic blend of ammonia and feces with which her fellow workers up the line must contend. A split-second pause and a quick glance up the line reveal an endless procession of chickens that seem to come faster and faster as the night wears on. There is little time to ponder whether her daughters are asleep in the bed they share in her mother's home.

Morning comes. Patricia drives home, tired enough to drop her entire body into bed. Instead, she makes breakfast, argues with her daughters over what they will wear to school, reminds them to get their books, sees them off to catch the bus, and sits down to watch some television to wind down. If Patricia is lucky she will be asleep by 10:00 A.M. and back up at 3:00 P.M., when the girls arrive home from school. Then it's after-school events, cleaning, laundry, and dinner.

A single mother, Patricia is better off than many in her small rural town, where women's median annual earnings are just above $13,000 and almost a third of the county population does not have a high school diploma. She does not receive child support, but at least she is able to live with her mother and she earns well above minimum wage. Still, even chicken-plant wages are not enough to allow her to support her daughters.

Six years later: Morning is half gone as Patricia pulls into the parking lot, turns off the engine, pulls the keys from the ignition of her new Ford Explorer, and enters the vintage clothing store. She might have come in earlier, but her daughter called from Germany and she did not want to rush her. Besides, her employees are extremely dependable. "They can handle the store," she thinks to herself. The day will be especially tedious as it is. It is inventory day and there are now more than four thousand items in her new consignment shop, the only one in her town.

Business has been especially good, and Patricia has had ample opportunity to put her business degree to work. "Life in general is good," she explains. It has been many years since the divorce. Both daughters are now grown, and Patricia is dating for the first time in years. She explains that her relationships are not too serious these days.

"I don't need a man but I do enjoy their company," she says, grinning.

Patricia might still be at the poultry plant today were it not for the head-on collision that left her severely injured. Besides a broken femur, she had to have a metal rod inserted in one leg, which, after several surgeries, left her with a two-inch bone loss. Because the poultry plant was the best-paying low-skill job for fifty miles, she knew that without an education, she and her daughters were doomed. The accident, she recalls, placed her on a leave of absence and, because of her inability to stand for a full shift, ultimately made her unable to return to the line. As a result, however, she became eligible for a "welfare-to-work" program that indirectly led her to college. Her caseworker told Patricia about a program titled "Project Success." Its purpose was to encourage single mothers to obtain job training or finish their educations. From there she learned about the Single Parent Scholarship Fund in her county, enrolled in college, and went on to earn a degree in business.

"Education is wasted on the youth," Patricia comments. She recalls how she became a sponge in college, absorbing everything she could. A first-generation college student, Patricia found that education changed her life significantly, and she is quick to assert, "There is no going back." Perhaps even more importantly, her daughters now know they will never have to settle for poverty. Patricia has provided them with the greatest gift of all: hope. As she looks out over the store she now owns, Patricia adds, "Growing up poor doesn't mean you have to die that way."

Sarah's background could not have been more different from Patricia's. Sarah grew up in New Orleans, the only child of well-educated parents who always expected her to obtain a college degree. She attended a girls' Catholic school and knew early on that she wanted to be an artist. Sarah's grandparents lived on farms, and she spent many of her summers with them helping in the garden and developing a love for animals, nature, and art. Now fifty-two years old, Sarah demonstrates her love for nature in exquisite watercolor paintings of the outdoors.

Sarah does not regret that a "back-to-the-land" wanderlust led her and her husband to a remote area in Arkansas in the 1970s. But as she explains, it did not take long for her husband to realize that he was not suited for country living. Meanwhile, Sarah remains firmly planted in the home that she and her four children have since built.

Today, all four of Sarah's children remain in the area. Since each child participated in the building of the house, Sarah is not surprised that they remain invested, emotionally and otherwise. The youngest just graduated from high school but still lives at home. They still have meals together on Sundays, especially during the summer, unless someone has other plans. They each share her artistic flair, and her love for nature and family rituals. The oldest son, now twenty-five, is building a house near his mother's on her forty-acre tract of land.

Sarah divorced in the early 1980s, and child support was minimal ($200 per month) when it came at all. As her children grew, the costs and time required for extracurricular activities ballooned. While she had hoped to find an outlet for her art so that she could continue to do it full-time, Sarah realized that single parenting required a steady income. In the beginning, living in poverty was not so bad, she remembers, but time was an issue. One of the most difficult things about being a single parent is needing to be two people at once. "For me," she explains, "time was the hardest, and then I chose to live a little further out, but it was a trade-off between a huge mortgage and driving. And for a while, when all the boys were a certain age, they were involved in sports or some extra-curricular activity. I mean, I must have driven that road thousands of times while I was raising them."

The life Sarah chose was not simple. She recalls, "We had to do everything. We had to cut our own wood. Everything that we could do, we did do. We did without if we couldn't do it ourselves, so it was tough, as far as managing time and being able to get out of any kind of survival mode."

In spite of her family background, when her marriage ended, Sarah was left, like most single mothers, struggling to make ends meet. Transportation, child care, and money for the kids' activities were difficult to obtain. She had no extended family to help, a resource single mothers are often forced to rely upon. For Sarah, this was not an option.

Fortunately, she had attended three years of college before her marriage, so returning to school was not as much a stretch for Sarah as it is for most poor single mothers. In the mid-1980s, she returned to school so that she would "have something to fall back on" if her art could not support her. "I've always been sort of academic," she explains. "I've always loved research and loved reading and knowing." Now, with a master's degree in education, Sarah can consider her options for the first time since her marriage.

Compared to many single parents, Sarah is an anomaly. While she struggled with self-esteem and having to ask for assistance, Sarah is able to look back on her situation as one of choice. Returning to school was a retooling experience. Money had not been a problem growing up. Unlike many of the women in this project, Sarah was exposed early on to the idea that college was a natural choice and was near finishing a degree when she married. However, what is remarkable and especially telling about Sarah's situation is that the conditions of divorce left her with the same dilemma other women face: how to make ends meet for her children. It was only after the divorce and the discovery that child support would not be forthcoming that Sarah realized her need to seek assistance and finish her education.

While single parenthood and poverty are separate phenomena, they are often found together. Regardless of their backgrounds, Sarah and Patricia have much in common. Their experiences are not isolated. Indeed, Sarah's unexpected loss of financial support provides evidence that poverty is a complex issue or, as Patricia explains, "It [poverty] ain't that simple." Further, the incidence of single parenthood is growing. In fact, single parent households have almost tripled in recent decades (from 9 percent of all households in 1960 to 25 percent in 1990).[1] In the 1990s, about 40 percent of single parent households were the result of divorce, while almost 31 percent of single household heads simply never married.[2] Not surprisingly, a huge majority (88 percent) of these families are female headed, and, as Table 1.1 reveals, many are poor. Thus, as both Patricia and Sarah demonstrate, regardless of how you reach single parenthood, the promise of a substantial

Table 1.1   U.S. Families and Female Householders with Incomes below the Poverty Line, 1998

Family Characteristic	Percentage
All families	10.0
White	8.0
Black	23.4
Hispanic origin (all races)	22.7
Asian and Pacific Islander	11.0
Female householder	29.9
White	24.9
Black	40.8
Hispanic origin (all races)	43.7
Asian and Pacific Islander	NA

Note: NA means not available.

Source: U.S. Bureau of the Census. 1998. "Poverty in the United States." *Current Population Reports,* Series P-60-215. Washington, D.C.: U.S. Government Printing Office. Available: http://www.census.gov/hhes/poverty.

loss in income and of continuing struggle patiently await your arrival.[3]

Then and Now: Welfare and the Single Parent Family

To speak honestly about the successes of the scholarship recipients requires some understanding of the hinterland of poverty from whence they came. Many of the single mothers who participated in the research for this book could not have finished their educations under current welfare law and the limitations of Clinton-era reforms.

With recent mandates to reduce welfare rolls, many more single parent families may be at risk of poverty. This is especially the case for single parents with little or no education and no marketable skills. For this group, the future looks especially bleak. Forced into low-wage jobs, many single parents will remain at risk of living in poverty long after they stop receiving aid. The trade-off is hardly appealing.

Welfare has an interesting past. Aid to Dependent Children (ADC), as it was originally called, was established in the 1930s during the Great Depression. Women with young children whose husbands had died, divorced them, or deserted them were considered "deserving" of public assistance. It was generally accepted that someone needed to be in the home full-time to nurture and care for the children, a value that has since become a luxury for many Americans. Preparing single mothers for the workforce was not a goal of the early programs. Even when the program was changed to Aid to Families with Dependent Children (AFDC) in the early 1960s, early supporters remained pro-family and wished to help mothers remain at home with their children.[4]

The social climate was different then. Social attitudes were more generous, even if the benefits were not. The number of welfare recipients had not yet grown to the level reached by the early 1990s (from approximately 5 million individuals in 1967 to approximately 14 million).[5] Women were not expected, much less encouraged, to compete with men in the workplace. Thus, women constituted only a small portion of the workforce. Moreover, the pay gap was such that women could only expect to earn about fifty-six cents to every dollar of their male counterparts compared to today's figure of about seventy-three cents.[6]

As the structure of American families changed, so too did attitudes toward welfare. Divorces increased dramatically, becoming what one sociologist described as "an acceptable remedy for the disappointment of our dreams."[7] At the same time, attitudes toward single mothers deteriorated. This was especially true for never-married mothers and even more so for African American women, the most visible group. There is great irony, according to sociologist William Julius Wilson, in the fact that, while most welfare recipients are white, African American women are more likely than their white female counterparts to be viewed as responsible for their own economic situations.[8] Prior to the 1960s, many states had strict regulations used to exclude African American children from benefits. Once the racist practices were ruled unconstitutional, more women of color were provided services. But the combination of racism and hostility toward out-of-wedlock births continued to add to the stigma. Images of "welfare queens" were perpetuated to convince the public that recipients were having babies in order to receive benefits, a myth still deeply entrenched in the nation's psyche.

Illegitimacy became the catch phrase for "moral breakdown." Single women as a group were no longer perceived as "deserving." Women now constituted almost half the workforce, and they were expected to obtain child care and gainful employment, regardless of their marital status or the ages of their children. Essentially, the value we once tenaciously upheld as a society, nurturing and caring for children, became a class issue. If you could afford to stay home with your children, then you should because it was good for them. But if you could not, the nurture ethic was replaced by the work ethic. In effect, the needs of children became overshadowed by the debate over the moral fabric of America, a controversy that is ongoing today.

Under current law (Public Law 104-193), the Temporary Assistance to Needy Families (TANF) program, which replaced AFDC, created procedures to move welfare recipients into the workplace. The stricter time limits for receiving benefits under the new program (a five-year lifetime allowance) have created a "black hole" into which many single parents are falling, especially in Arkansas where the state limits participation to two years. As in most states, Arkansas recipients must work after two years, with few exceptions. While some beneficiaries have been able to receive adequate job training in this time period, many—especially those attempting to acquire an education, a proven route to self-sufficiency—are being cut off and forced into employment midway through their schooling. Embedded in this system of welfare is a great irony: Many of the jobs obtained do not provide a living wage and thus cannot raise a family's standard of living above the poverty level. This is especially the case for women and people of color, who already earn less than their male counterparts in any job.[9]

Another irony is that by taking jobs that pay at or just above the minimum wage (currently $5.15 per hour), former welfare recipients lose important benefits such as health care insurance and child care assistance. This is true even with transition programs: unless the jobs pay far above minimum wage, recipients will fall through the safety net and have to struggle with the inadequate benefits provided by low-wage jobs. President Clinton recognized this paradox when he stated, "There are things that keep people on welfare. One is the tax burden of low wage work; another is the cost of child care; another is the cost of medical care . . . today you have this bizarre situation where people on welfare, if they take a job in a place which doesn't offer health insurance, are asked to give up their children's health care and go to work. . . . That doesn't make any sense."[10]

Single mothers throughout Arkansas echoed this sentiment and provided vivid examples of what this contradiction has meant in their own lives. The barriers they encountered included everything from rising child care costs and inadequate transportation to insufficient child support. Moreover, being a single mother also means bracing oneself against the punitive rhetoric and hyperbole of conservative politicians and the diminished self-esteem that grinding poverty brings. It means struggling to make ends meet, sometimes against great odds. Perhaps most important, being a single parent means looking for employment that pays enough to pull your family out of poverty. This is no easy task in the South.[11] Indeed, it is a long shot in a place where the realities associated with single parenting are especially sobering.

For the children of these families, living in a single mother household means a tenfold increase in the likelihood of living in poverty and being twice as likely as nonpoor children to fail in school. It means having slower than average cognitive development and experiencing poorer health than children from families who are better off. Growing up in poverty means a higher likelihood of experiencing learning and behavioral problems and a lower chance of being read to by an adult.[12]

Living in poverty means a much higher chance of experiencing malnutrition. The rural poor are over 65 percent more likely than the non-poor to maintain an inadequate diet, one lacking a variety of essential nutrients. The outlook is especially bleak for the rural South, found to be the region with "the highest prevalence of biochemical deficiencies."[13] The "worst" it is said is "saved for last—infant mortality and low birth weight."[14] The despair of poverty, hunger, and malnutrition in the South, combined with its higher levels of infant mortality, cause one to ponder whether the region is not a separate entity indeed. And while these figures are true for poor children everywhere, whether they receive welfare or not, the conditions that lead to them are most prevalent in the South; the U.S. Census Bureau reports that the South contains all but one of the 10 poorest states in the nation.

2 Barriers to Success

Unfortunately, there are no books one can read to prepare for the journey into poverty, and far too many single mothers entered their divorces thinking, "We may have our differences, but he will want to do the right thing for the children's sake." Life should be so simple!

Contrary to popular belief, there are few safety nets for those at the bottom. Margaret, a mother of five, has been homeless twice. Both times she and her children became homeless, she was working a full-time job. Margaret has since earned a master's degree in education and earns almost double the median income for women in Arkansas today. Still, just talking about her experiences hits a raw nerve. Like most of the mothers in this book, Margaret remembers her struggles excruciatingly well. She recalls with a mixture of humor and sarcasm, "For me, falling into the 'safety net' would have been like falling into the lap of luxury."

For too many, life after divorce means dealing with the anger and disappointment of learning that your ex-spouse has adopted an "out of sight, out of mind" approach to parenting. While welfare reform was supposed to include better child-support enforcement, the reality has been very different. The women in this study found child support extremely difficult to obtain and even harder to keep. Their experiences reflect those of single parents throughout the United States.

21

The proportion of single parents receiving all the child support payments they were due increased from 34 percent in 1993 to 41 percent in 1997. Single mothers received a greater proportion of the total child support due than did single fathers (60 percent versus 48 percent). Of the estimated 14 million single parents having custody of 22.9 million children under the age of 21, however, 85 percent were women. This means that 85 percent of single parents received only 60 percent of all child support, and that roughly 7.8 million of the 19.5 million children lived in single mother households that received no support.[1]

In theory, reforms in child-support enforcement are a positive step, with their provisions for establishing paternity and automatic withdrawal of support payments from fathers' wages. However, while welfare laws are aimed at increased accountability for non-custodial parents, most of the women in this book received little to no support from the fathers of their children. Absent parents often move frequently, and keeping track of them is difficult. Regina, a mother of three, is quick to talk about the disappearance phenomenon. As she explained, "He paid once or twice and gave up on it. He's very conveniently disappeared off the face of the earth. I don't think he's dead," she says with little emotion, "but nobody knows where he is. The state of Georgia just got in touch with me because that was the last place he'd been located. They said, 'We haven't been able to find him. We're giving up on it.'" She concludes matter-of-factly, "That's the way it goes with child support."

Similarly, Sarah has tried to collect child support since her son was two years old. He is now eighteen and will

soon enter college. Her dealings with child-support enforcement have left her bitter. Like Regina, Sarah does not
know where the absent father is. "In eighteen years, you'd
think that they [the welfare authorities] could accomplish
something," she says angrily. "It was like they were incompetent. They *were* incompetent! Never got anything done,
and how much was it?" she asks, and then answers herself:
"One hundred and fifty dollars. And you know, he owes
now, after eighteen years, about twenty thousand dollars,
or something like that. Rick is going to college next year. It
would help him so much."

Sarah is not angry just at her ex-spouse. She is equally
angry with the system. "I'd like to say, 'You know, you take
the welfare away from the mothers, but at the same time
you don't collect anything from the fathers.' This picture is
not right. It seems to me in eighteen years they could have
done something. They could have done something."

The idea that both parents should share responsibility
for their children, even after divorce, is a noble goal.
However, many non-custodial parents (mostly fathers) are
also poor and lack the means to fulfill their responsibility.
Some sociologists argue that "insisting on [compliance]
without effectively creating the conditions for them to
meet their obligations will only redistribute the poverty of
female-headed families to include those non-custodial parents."[2] The result is no real change for either.

Perhaps there is merit to this argument, even though it
creates felt ambivalence among those most sympathetic.
Research has shown that the rate of unemployment
among unskilled men is now twice that of the national average. Moreover, the percentage of males aged twenty-five

to thirty-four who earn less than enough to lift a family above the poverty line has more than doubled since 1969. As Karen Seccombe points out, simply to blame the absent father may do little to "encourage the creation of realistic interventions designed to ameliorate this national problem."[3] Poverty does not excuse the absence of non-custodial support, but it clearly points out the complexity of the issue.

Terri has a four-year-old son whose health problems prevented him from staying in a public day-care setting. Terri was forced to seek private care for her son. However, when she found a private sitter with only a few children in her university apartment complex (Terri has no vehicle), she was unable to receive financial help with child care. The loss of child-care assistance created a huge barrier for Terri as she struggled to remain in school. She recalls her dilemma:

> It's like when you're on the welfare system. They only allow up to $175 per month to be counted on what you pay out of your pocket for day care. Whereas, I was putting out $280 a month, not counting the food. Just $280 a month in day care expenses. That's a car payment. That's one heck of a car payment. The system right now, as it's set up, actually works against people trying to get on their feet. . . . You figure, I spent, in the three and one-half years I've been here, not counting the short time he was in regular day care that I got assistance, I probably spent about $6,000 out of my pocket on day care.

This figure is in line with national averages, especially given that Terri is referring only to part-time child-care costs. Researchers report that the average cost for the care of one preschool-age child ranged from three to eight thousand dollars per year.[4] Unfortunately, child care is also becoming more scarce, not just in Arkansas but nation-wide. High quality, affordable child care is especially diffi-cult to obtain. Child care during evenings, overnight, and on weekends is even more scarce. And special-needs chil-dren—that is, those with disabilities who require special at-tention—are at an even greater disadvantage.[5] These trends have important implications, inasmuch as research has shown that high-quality care is positively related to IQ scores and leads to fewer behavioral problems. Conversely, poor care has been associated with lower academic per-formance, slower cognitive development, and behavioral problems through at least the second grade.[6]

Single mothers also complained that the welfare system sent mixed messages. While the cash assistance averages only 60 percent of the poverty line, the opportunity to sup-plement the aid with cash income is greatly limited by re-strictive guidelines.[7] As a result, many single mothers felt stuck before they were provided the opportunity to finish their education. Some charged the system with being irra-tional. Penny, a single parent for over sixteen years, was quick to identify welfare as the most important barrier fac-ing single parents today. With more than a little agitation, she explained:

> Well for one thing, the biggest barrier is the welfare system. . . . The thing about it is after my divorce, I went to try and get help just with housing and food stamps. I had a job. I worked for ———— merchandiser. I worked in the office, was making above minimum wage, but I couldn't get any help. I made too much money. *Excuse me!* By the time I paid child care, gas and food, there was nothing left. Simply nothing. And they had the nerve to tell me that if I chose to quit and stay home, I could get this, this, and this. So, instead of

helping people, they make people dependent on the system
because they punish them if they try to get ahead . . . punish
them if they're working or making any money.

Penny was so angry over her experience that she wrote to
her Congressman and Senators to complain about the situation. She laughs as she finishes her story: "By the time
they got my letter I was laid off and was eligible for all the
services."

Penny's perceptions were somewhat misguided, but the
mixed messages she received seem common.[8] Various restrictions and limitations on public assistance seemed to be
problematic in many areas. In addition to child care and resource restrictions, transportation seemed to be a problem
for some. Karen, a single mother for five years, recalls, "If
you happen to have a vehicle and it's worth over a certain
amount, they can deny you on that. My point to them was
if I have a good vehicle, then I have transportation. It
seemed to me that they were telling me through all the
rules and regulations, not them personally, that I had to
have a yucky car in order to get assistance while I was
going to school."

In 1997 Laura's car blew up, and she had to purchase a
new car with her student loan. The purchase cost Laura her
welfare benefits. The trade-off was worth it, she explains,
but it left her perplexed:

> I wanted a new car because I knew I'd be driving to work,
> and I wanted a nice, dependable car. When you own a new
> car, though, you get no benefits from social services. You
> can only have assets valued no more than $2,500. They
> don't take into consideration that when you buy a car that
> you don't really buy the car—you have another bill. . . .
> It's a little backwards. You're supposed to buy a car for

$700–$800 and then put $1,000 into it for repairs. You never
know when you wake up in the morning whether it's going
to start, whether it's going to break down on the road.
Obviously, you would prefer not to do that. You'd prefer
to have a car that was dependable. I never could figure
that out.[9]

Federal regulations under the TANF program left much
flexibility for states to use block-grant monies to customize
their own welfare laws. In Arkansas, Act 1058 (the Arkansas Personal Responsibility and Public Assistance Reform
Act) was designed to eliminate welfare as "a permanent
way of life." As the title illustrates, current Arkansas law
reflects both the moral and monetary concerns of the
state's General Assembly. Concern over long-term dependency is highlighted in the purpose statement:

> This system of continuous income maintenance not only discourages all incentive for an individual to become self-sufficient, but often leads to intergenerational dependency, and
> has built-in disincentives toward obtaining work and toward
> any effort to seek and secure a job. The total package of welfare benefits available to some is frequently better than the
> package of benefits the working poor can obtain, creating an
> incentive to stay on welfare.

But a paradox exists in the stated objective of welfare
today—to help recipients become able to take work that is
available to them. The jobs for which low-skilled workers
most often qualify are those with the lowest pay and the
fewest benefits. Thus, the argument in the purpose statement above is only partially correct. For example, one
study found that single mothers who earned between five
and seven dollars per hour experienced more material
hardship than those who received welfare.[10] Careful analy-

sis of these conditions, in fact, constitutes a strong argument for raising the poverty threshold. Research on what a family needs in order to cover basic budget items (food, rent, clothing, child care, transportation, and the like), reveals that the official cut-off points are too low. A basic budget for a single-parent family with two children calls for an income of over $30,000 in 1996 dollars,[11] a figure more than twice the current poverty threshold. Families who are forced to make do with cash allowances *below* the poverty level experience real hardship and unmet needs for child care, transportation, housing, health insurance, over-the-counter medicines, and prescriptions.[12] Again, the trade-off is hardly appealing.

Perhaps the overly zealous focus upon the welfare population has diverted our attention away from the pervasiveness of low-wage work. The cart seems to have been put before the horse. In other words, structural changes that lead to real living wages must be in place to alleviate poverty, for both those receiving welfare and those who do not. But perhaps the social critics are right. Maybe eliminating poverty is a lesser goal to Americans than reduction of the welfare rolls.[13]

Transitional programs are in place. In Arkansas, for example, Transitional Employment Assistance (TEA) is designed to support former AFDC clients in their attempts to become gainfully employed, either through education or training. The education component, however, has been restrictive and limited, and receives far less emphasis than the work component. Instead, tax incentives and matched wages are in place to persuade businesses to employ former welfare recipients. Community service programs are also in place, whereby recipients can work at no cost to the participating agency while they continue receiving benefits. Other incentives are also available for work. For example, child-care assistance can be paid for during the first year of employment and then on a sliding scale for the second and third years. Some work-related expenses, such as for materials and supplies, can be reimbursed, although there is a $200 lifetime limit.

Some can qualify for medical insurance for up to a year after starting employment. However, not everyone who is eligible takes advantage of this option. One report revealed that many of those exiting welfare do not receive private health insurance in their new jobs. And while children are automatically eligible for public health benefits, some mothers may also obtain up to one year of transitional coverage but many do not know about this option. Once their cases are closed because of employment, many do not realize that they remain eligible and can reapply for medical coverage. In other words, coverage is not automatic and does not transfer easily. The onus is on the recipient to reapply.

Realistically speaking, what incentive is there for caseworkers to inform clients of this option? States can qualify for huge federal grants just for showing evidence of reduced welfare enrollment. In some cases, the bonus is as high as $20 million, to be used as the state sees fit. And while Arkansas law requires that recipients be notified of transitional child care and Medicaid benefits, several of the women in this study were not given that option. As critics like Julie Rodman argue, not only does closing cases "leave [women and their families] unprotected, but it also threatens welfare reform and the overall health-care treatment system."[14]

Recent innovative legislation in Arkansas seeks to correct this oversight. The revised welfare-reform law, enacted in 1999, places greater emphasis on education and training and requires that supportive services be provided while clients are participating in either component. The education component includes basic education, vocational education or training, and college. The new law requires that caseworkers provide a minimum of seven hundred clients the opportunity to gain vocational training and four hundred clients the opportunity to attend college. Individuals enrolled full-time in coursework are required to work an additional fifteen hours per week.[15]

While the new requirements are a step toward promoting true self-sufficiency, single parents remain disadvantaged, given that every hour spent in class typically requires at least one and a half to two hours of study. For non-traditional students, the study time required is often much longer. A student enrolled in twelve to fifteen hours of courses can be expected to invest from thirty-five to fifty hours a week toward her education. Meeting the requirement for another fifteen hours of paid work leaves very little time for home and children. Finally, while this change in legislation is certainly better than the alternative, it has yet to become widespread policy.

Transitional health insurance and child-care benefits help, but they do not go far enough. Once these temporary programs end, the safety net will rip open once again, and families will fall through as they attempt to meet their basic needs. And while increases in the 1990s to the minimum wage and the federal Earned Income Tax Credit (EITC) help, more long-term changes are needed in the lives of women and their children in order to see any marked improvement in self-sufficiency.

The dramatic decrease in welfare caseloads throughout the nation, and especially in Arkansas,[16] obscures the fact that, without decent jobs, former recipients are bound to remain in or near poverty. The lifetime limitations on benefits may also put poor children, whose poverty rates have risen faster than any other group in the past two decades, even more at risk than they already are. The issue of child poverty throughout the United States is staggering: in a country possessing over $15 trillion in wealth, four out of every ten people in poverty are children under eighteen years of age.[17] This figure translates into almost one in five children (18.7 percent) in the United States living in poverty, and more than half of them reside in female-headed households.[18] These statistics are double the equivalent figures for Canada and ten times higher than those of Sweden.[19] When we consider race and ethnicity as well, the figures become even more dramatic. Among all children in the United States under the age of eighteen, 19.2 percent lived in poverty in 1997. Yet just 15.4 percent of white children lived below the line, compared to 36.4 percent of Hispanic children and 36.8 percent of African American children.[20]

Among female-headed Latino families, 72 percent of children under the age of six live in poverty. For African American children in the same age category, 73 percent of those in female-headed households remain in poverty.[21] Poverty in our country is hardly a random event. Yet when we search for causes, we find ourselves tangled in the rhetoric of individualism.

3 Myths and Images

The Morality Trap

Ideologically, it seems that it is not so important to us, as Americans, that we all be equal, as it is that we all have equal opportunities. These views often boil down to individual theories of shame and blame. If the world in fact worked as we would like to believe, Americans could count on rewards matching investment. In other words, the harder we work, and the more perseverance and ambition we demonstrate, the greater will be our reward. When we achieve success, we give ourselves the credit. When we fail, we blame ourselves. This thinking appeals to us because it seems neither complicated nor unfair; poor people are poor simply because they are not trying as hard as the rest of us. Popular notions reflect these images.[1] After all, we all know someone who applied himself or herself and "made" it.

Opinion polls bear this out. For example, in 1990 the National Opinion Research Center (NORC) found that 40 percent of Americans believed too much was being spent on welfare. By 1994, that number had risen to 65 percent.[2] The AFDC program was strongly criticized for costing too much, even though it accounted for only about 1 percent of the federal budget.[3] In other words, combined expenditures for AFDC, food stamps, and Medicaid total approximately $117 billion per year.[4] On the other hand, "wealth-

33

fare" or "aid to dependent corporations" cost taxpayers an estimated $730 billion over a five-year period from 1995 to 2000. Broken down, that means $146 billion in aid to the rich versus $117 billion for a combination of services to the poor. Moreover, in the mid-1990s, Citizens for Tax Justice reported that corporations were enjoying tax breaks that equaled an estimated $200 billion and that a few hundred large corporations were benefiting from the bulk of the savings. Property and estate tax deductions, charitable contributions, and mortgage interest deductions all serve to benefit those in the upper-middle and upper classes disproportionately. Current tax reform by the Bush administration has been criticized for benefiting only the wealthiest families in the United States. In other words, tax loopholes for the very rich and corporations are entitlement programs that remain largely invisible to American taxpayers.[5]

Another myth, which I find difficult to dispel in my sociology classes, is that welfare mothers get into the welfare system and stay there. In fact, according to some studies, two-thirds of those who received AFDC benefits exited the programs within two years. Only 9 percent stayed for more than seven years, and less than 10 percent stayed more than eight years.[6] Until the 1996 welfare reform, those most likely to have lengthy stays on welfare were young single mothers with children under the age of three.

Single mothers are especially sensitive to this myth. In an earlier research project, I learned that welfare-to-work participants wanted others to know that their tenure on public assistance was short. This belief that assistance should be as brief as possible resonated with me because I remember having set a deadline for myself. I wanted to be able to say that I had received food stamps for less than a year. That somehow made it seem more temporary. The longer I needed assistance, the more I came to identify myself as a welfare recipient, an identity I very much wanted to avoid.

The myth that welfare mothers have too many children is equally popular. Arkansas politicians were so concerned about this issue that they enacted a measure referred to as the "family cap." It denies additional money to women if they have children while on welfare. The first problem with this myth is that 84 percent of TANF single parents have just one or two children, the average for the general population. Second, the notion that welfare is too generous and that women have children in order to increase their welfare payments, frankly, makes no sense. Allowances for additional births range from $27 to $147 per child, depending upon the state of residence, figures that do not begin to match the expense of an additional child.[7]

Another persistent myth is that the children of welfare mothers will become welfare users themselves. Deena, a social worker with a twenty-year-old son, explained to me how she worried about being on welfare because she wanted her son to have a strong work ethic. "I was particularly concerned with that," she explained, "because I had public assistance, and I didn't want him to be a second generation on public assistance."

For the small proportion of children who later go on welfare themselves, situational factors such as employment difficulties, spousal non-support, and transportation problems may better explain continued use than the more popular perceptions of moral corruption or laziness. I have always been perplexed by the sarcasm attached to public discussions of intergenerational poverty. Perhaps the rhetoric surrounding this particular myth is so harsh because children are at the center of the debate. Comments made by legislators while hashing out the 1988 Family Support Act, which became law under President Reagan, reflect this attitude: "This legislation is designed to reach those children of welfare mothers who grow up learning more about the welfare office than an employment office. . . . A reform with mandatory participation will break the welfare dependency cycle in those families who prefer a welfare check to a paycheck."[8]

This kind of thinking is in many ways flawed. Even poor families not on welfare struggle to provide a safe, nurturing environment for their children. Research shows that when education and routine structure (a near impossibility for poor single parents) and access to regular health care are present, children fare much better, even in poorest families.[9] Despite that in Arkansas the proportion of children living in poverty went from 27.4 percent in 1979 to 16.3 percent in 1998, programs are still needed to serve children entering school, who require health care, child care services, and nutritional support.[10] Indeed, some research has found that children in families receiving welfare are at least able to obtain somewhat routine medical and dental care.[11] If it is the children for whom we are concerned, state programs must build upon this knowledge and provide permanent change via education and create real potential for living wages.

Even more myths abound. For example, there is the notion that most welfare recipients are African American teenage mothers who live in inner cities. In fact, most welfare recipients are white, although the proportion who are

African American is higher than their representation in the general population since they are much poorer as a group.[12]

Louise, an African American single mother and former scholarship recipient who was once on welfare, is now working toward her master's degree in education. She remains excruciatingly aware of the welfare stigma. Although it has been two years since Louise received any assistance, she explains, "I'm really still embarrassed about it. I know what people say, but I didn't have a choice." Many women shared Louise's insight, realizing that popular sentiment creates a double stigma for women who are both black and poor.

Another popular myth depicts welfare recipients as lazy. Yet in 1994, 18 percent of full-time incomes remained below the poverty level and 50 percent of all families in poverty were headed by someone who worked. One-third of those worked full-time jobs.[13] Moreover, AFDC had such strict limits that many women feared losing their benefits if they earned money in addition to their monthly stipends. Their fears were not unfounded. Julie, a mother of two, remembers, "If I earned any cash I kept my mouth shut, and there was always a sense of anxiety or, I guess, guilt. You couldn't be just poor. You had to be dirt poor."

Martha was one of those who worked full-time but remained poor. She has three children, two grown and one still at home. Martha remembers when she was earning too much to qualify for food stamps. "When I worked for the health department," she explained, "I made too much to get food stamps because I made about eight hundred dollars a month and by it being just the two of us, I could have gotten eight or nine dollars [in food stamps] a month, but it wasn't worth all the paperwork and all of the time I had to spend down there [at the social services office]."

As most Americans understand, $800 per month is hardly enough to cover housing and utility costs, much less clothing, child care, transportation, health care, and other living expenses. But the system used to measure poverty has changed little since it was established during the Johnson administration, nearly 40 years ago.[14] Today, the Census Bureau provides statistics on those within 125 percent of the official poverty level, a far more realistic measurement given the numerous increases in non-food costs. When we add this group, the number of those in poverty is close to 18 percent.[15]

Why are these false and damaging stereotypes so enduring? As I talked with women throughout the state of Arkansas, I wondered if perhaps it has to do with our own fears. Perhaps it is too frightening to acknowledge that even though some people are trying their best, they still slip through the safety net. It simply does not fit the American dream. It seems that we hold strongly to the egalitarian ethos that we all have the same ability and opportunity for upward mobility, but when success eludes us, for whatever reason, the blame game begins.

What surprised me most during my research was the degree to which so many of the women shared these images of themselves. In retrospect, I should have anticipated this. After all, the negative messages about welfare carry with them a surge of moral legitimation from the media to politicians to even the clergy. By this, I mean that the popular images brought forth are jam-packed with justifications that are largely taken for granted. For example, even though many welfare recipients work at least part time, they are seen as lacking in initiative. Opinion polls reveal that "lack of effort" is the typical explanation for welfare dependence. Yet most of these women worked at full-time jobs before they returned to school, and each of them made at or near poverty wages. Like more than 13 million other Americans, they were trapped in the "low-wage twilight zone."[16]

Resisting the cultural scripts and the inclination to blame oneself is difficult. "I think it comes from inside you," says Madonna, a mother of five. "I just know the things I heard from my family. I know the rhetoric I hear on television about generations of recipients, yada yada." But even though Madonna worked full-time, she still qualified for food stamps to feed her family. "If I just got paid better," she continued. "Why is my life not worth as much as someone who does something that I don't do? It's not exactly my fault. What is my fault, if you can call it a fault, is that I've got five children." Madonna's ambivalence was reflected time and time again by others who faced the same dilemmas.

While the women were susceptible to the popular notions, they seemed to be able to separate themselves from them, referring more often to "circumstances" than "lack of effort." The effect was what sociologists describe as role distancing—attempting to ensure that they were not confused with a "typical" welfare recipient.[17] Martha, for example, considered herself very different from the stereotype:

> Certain single parents survive by being single parents. There are some that say, "Well, I can get this and the government will take care of us. And they'll give us food stamps and we can get a house to move into." And that's how they survive

by not wanting to work. And that's the ones that give us a
bad name.

Martha did not know that other single mothers, like herself, were struggling with full-time jobs. She just knew that
she was doing it "by the book" and, just as Madonna found,
it was not enough.

Sarah was especially quick to distance herself from the
stereotype. As she put it, she was not so concerned for herself as she was for "typical" single mothers:

> I had a brain. I always had options. Somehow, I've always
> managed to keep a roof over our head and a decent car to
> drive. But think of all the women who have no cars to drive
> and no sense, and may be a little retarded or something.
> Those children, I mean, what are those children going to
> grow up with? They don't even know how to feed them.

Many of the women in the study saw themselves as
atypical. At first I worried that this attitude might give
them a distorted view of themselves and their circumstances. But over time I began to understand their attempts
to distance themselves from others. They had become war-
riors in a battle to survive the barrage of stigmatizing rhetoric. This was their only defense. Karen Seccombe deals ex-
tensively with this subject in her study of welfare
recipients' perceptions of welfare. She writes:

> Social arrangements, which are in the best interest of the
> dominant group, are presented as being in everyone's best in-
> terests. Subordinates come to accept these interests as their
> own, and the contradictions inherent in the interests of the
> dominant and subordinate groups are ignored. Thus, the
> ideology becomes "common sense" and normative, and cohe-
> sion is created where there would otherwise be conflict. The
> ideologies reflect the interests and perspectives of the elite, but

the poor, who fail to see the shared political nature of their problems, also internalize them.[18]

Poverty, a social phenomenon, becomes relegated to the realm of personal problems.

The moral overtones become heavy and difficult to battle as critics argue that by eliminating welfare and government aid to single parents, we can better help them to achieve self-sufficiency.[19] Unless a person has experienced the deep isolation of poverty, and the diminished self-esteem it brings, it is difficult to appreciate the power of such punitive rhetoric.

Laura shared the same ambivalence about asking for public assistance, but knew she had to provide for her two sons. "I felt like pond scum," she remembered, "but that didn't deter me from asking." Indeed, each of the women felt the social stigma in very personal ways. Laura's comment resonated with me personally. I, too, remember feeling my self-worth plummet in settings where I felt guilty for having to receive assistance. It was only after I began to study sociology that I realized the power that being labeled a "welfare mother" had over me.

Social labels are important. Particular kinds can have negative influence and seriously alter our self-concepts when our identities are discredited.[20] Moreover, attacks on our selves are especially destructive when we are powerless to combat them.

Interestingly, for these women the most memorable examples of humiliation took place in a public setting most of us would consider neutral territory—the grocery store. A trip to the grocery store with what Sonya's child called "funny money" transforms the store into a public setting for rituals of self-degradation, in part because the stigma becomes visible the moment one presents food stamps at the check-out counter. "You definitely feel people giving you dirty looks and staring at you when you're paying for things with food stamps," Rene recalls. She learned to avoid certain cashiers and remembers once having to go to the post office to pick up her food stamp allotment. "Every so often they would send it certified mail, I guess just to make sure the right person was getting it. The guy working behind the counter [was] being real friendly until he came back with what he knew was food stamps . . . and being very cold when he handed them to me. There's definitely stigma attached."

"Being a food-stamp recipient in the community is a difficult thing," Laura told me. "You go to Wal-Mart and stock up your cart with groceries and you're consciously thinking, 'OK, if I get in front of some bozo, are they going to be going "blah blah" because I've got this name brand instead of generic? Or, what are they going to think if I get this family pack of steaks or whatever?' That's happened before," she continues. "I was paying for groceries with food stamps, and there was a bozo behind me that ran into me with his cart. Hit my back with his cart, the whole time I was standing there with my food stamps out!" As the object of such stigma you can never be sure how to interpret other people's responses to you. Laura explained, "When you get a grumpy checker, it could be that the person is having a bad day, but you're going to interpret it as your fault for using food stamps." Similarly, Karen, a mother of two, remembers having to give herself pep talks when she entered the store, thinking, "OK, Karen, just be brave. I don't care what other people think. This is getting me through school."

Children are not immune to the stigma either. Once Sonya was in the store with her daughter. She was paying for their groceries with her food stamps when her daughter said, "Mama, what kind of funny money is that?" "Both of us laughed in the store," she recalls. But in reality, she remembers that each trip to the store left her "trying to hurry up and sneak in and use it hoping that nobody saw me." Sandra remembers that her daughter became more and more embarrassed each time, no doubt sensing her mother's humiliation.

Magdalene's children would disappear during the actual transactions. "My kids, when we went grocery shopping, we'd get in line to pay for it and they would go sit in the car. They would not be seen in there with me paying for that with food stamps. I would go to Harrison to get my groceries so people in Jasper wouldn't see me with them" (food stamps).

The stigma felt by these women is part of the morality trap that many Americans fall into when they become financially dependent upon the government. But as some critics point out, we often forget that the system of welfare and the phenomenon of single parenting are hardly gender-neutral. To state, as one Congressman did, "If there's a minimum wage job out there, we expect you to take it," is to ignore the real needs and concerns of poverty and instead to adopt a punitive, moralistic stance that fails to recognize the difficulties that working mothers face with respect to child care, health care, child support, and the workplace. [21] Karen Seccombe writes: "[T]hese discussions [of welfare reform] are problematic because they assume that welfare is a gender neutral program. It is not. Recipients are predominantly women, and the needs and concerns embedded in women's real life experiences as caretakers of children are not contextualized within their recommendations to reduce or eliminate welfare."[22]

Maintaining a consistent self-image over time requires social support.[23] And because our culture values ambition and hard work, we see those who are struggling as somehow deficient while those who "make it" are held in great esteem. We hold tightly to the "rags to riches" stories in our culture, however rare they may be. Wealthy people are assumed to have succeeded because they simply tried harder than everyone else; thus they must possess a stronger work ethic. We have our American heroes: the Horatio Alger types like Sam Walton or Bill Gates. They are believed to be more willing to take risks and possess drives that are unique to hard-working individuals. If you are a successful person, you are also likely to develop feelings of self-efficacy, that is, a belief that your own actions bring rewards. The process is circular: those with higher rewards elicit more respect from others, which in turn legitimates their status and makes it easier to reject negative social labels and manage the impressions of others.

Finally, there is the good old-fashioned "luck of the draw," otherwise known as fatalism.[24] This equally simplistic view has always been one of my favorites. After all, who among us has not had visions of waking up to find the Publisher's Clearinghouse van parked in our driveway, or buying that one lucky lottery ticket? Believing in luck implies that much of what happens to us is really fate. We are poor or wealthy because of luck. Our relative positions in life are nothing more than "quirks of birth, human nature, chance and related forces," each beyond our control.[25]

Growing up in the same small town as Sam Walton, I have seen first-hand that being in the right place at the right time can bring a huge payoff. When I was a child, my mother often said, "Everything that happens to us has a purpose. Things don't happen without a reason." But it was also my mother who told me, "Part of life is what happens, and the rest is how you deal with it." Taken separately, her comments have contradictory meanings; but taken together, they hold great wisdom. Being born poor is indeed a condition of fate. Remaining poor may be better understood through what sociologists describe as "structural" explanations.

Using a sociological framework, we are forced to acknowledge that poverty is more than an individual problem. Rather, there are patterns to this phenomenon. We find that welfare dependency is hardly gender-neutral, inasmuch as women and children largely constitute the poor. The fact that some segments of society are more likely to be poor than others begs an investigation of the economic and social factors that disadvantage entire groups.

I have found in my college teaching experience that to talk about children in poverty is one thing, but I need only mention the terms "welfare" and "discrimination" and most students tune out. This holds even though most "welfare" recipients are children. Perhaps the resistance is due to the fact that in today's race- and class-segregated world, the middle class and wealthy do not ordinarily interact with the poor, while the working class cannot afford to. First, they are too busy trying to keep themselves out of poverty. Second, if they examine poverty too closely, it might reveal the false hopes to which many in the working class necessarily cling. Their own springboards to higher-

Table 3.1 Mean Household Income and Share of Aggregate Income by Quintile, 1998

Quintile	Mean Household Income (dollars)	Share of Aggregate Household Income (percentage)
Lowest fifth	9,223	3.6
Second fifth	23,288	9.0
Third fifth	38,967	15.0
Fourth fifth	60,266	23.2
Highest fifth	127,529	49.2

Source: Mean household income figures from U.S. Bureau of the Census. 1998. "Money Income of Households, Families, and Persons in the United States: 1998." *Current Population Reports,* Series P-60. Washington, D.C.: U.S. Government Printing Office. Share of aggregate income from U.S. Bureau of the Census. 1998. "Household Wealth and Asset Ownership: 1998." *Current Population Reports,* Series P-70. Washington, D.C.: U.S. Government Printing Office.

paying jobs may not be broken, but they are seriously cracked. When we consider the distribution of household incomes among Americans, we see that a small proportion earns most of the income (see Table 3.1).

As Table 3.1 reveals, while the median annual income for the wealthiest fifth of the American populace was $127,529 in 1998, the poorest fifth had to get by on $9,223. The stock market boom of the 1990s failed to benefit many hard-working American citizens, 34 million of whom can be officially classified as poor.[26] The current official system for measuring poverty has been challenged on a number of points. Critics argue that a more realistic measure would significantly raise the number of those counted as poor.

In 1995 the National Academy of Sciences published a report from a panel that had studied the official poverty measures that have been in place since 1969. Among the recommendations to emerge from the study were that the poverty threshold should be adjusted to better represent the costs of food, clothing, shelter (including utilities), everyday needs, child-care costs, medical out-of-pocket expenses, work-related costs, and cost-of-living variations based on geographic location. The study also recommended that the measure should count the value of in-kind benefits, such as food stamps, subsidized housing, school lunches, and home energy assistance. [27] The federal Office of Management and Budget encouraged the Bureau of the Census to provide experimental poverty figures to reflect these recommendations. Using these measures, the rate of poverty is, not surprisingly, significantly higher—as high as 18 percent, as mentioned earlier.

Finally, as sociologist C. Wright Mills argued, when a social phenomenon affects significant segments of a population, it is no longer a personal trouble but instead becomes a social issue. Let us consider, then, the phenomenon of poor children, the most vulnerable of the poor. Statistics reveal that poor children tend to have lower academic achievement than other children. It is true that they are more likely to drop out of school, become parents in adolescence, and be jobless. And they are more likely to suffer health problems, including low birth weight, malnutrition, sudden infant death, and birth defects.[28] Poor children are more likely to be victims of homicide and suicide.[29] They are more likely to be neglected and to suffer serious injury from abuse.[30] Children of the poor are more likely to experience social withdrawal, depression, and low self-esteem, and to suffer from various behavioral disorders.[31]

Interventions are needed to help reduce the "cycle of poverty," but these must come in the form of opportunities that can actually reduce the incidence of poverty. Punitive measures do not move people out of poverty. If anything, they disarm poor people, making them less able to cope with an already enormous task of survival. At best, the welfare reform measures currently in place transform the poor into the "working poor" but seldom reduce the odds against them. What researchers agree on, however, is that there is continued promise when education is a key ingredient. But first it has to be accessible.

4 Education and Mobility

I often teach a course called Social Class in America. Over the period of a semester we grapple with many aspects of social inequality, but perhaps the most difficult challenge is getting students past the notion that we live in a classless society. The egalitarian ethos is strong in our culture, and students often accept it without any measure of skepticism. As we move through the semester, together we attempt to get beyond the ideology of equality and equip ourselves to contemplate the old saying, "It's easy to climb the ladder of social mobility when your parents own the ladder!" But what other factors influence the process of social mobility?

Poverty and the distribution of wealth are class issues, admittedly complicated by race and gender. We are born into a particular social class, and most of us will die in the same one into which we were born. While some will rise above our class origins, many more—equally conscientious, willing, and able—will remain in poverty.

I typically spend a third or more of the semester talking about sociological theories that explain stratification (that is, systematic patterns of inequality) in society. But a clear approach to the paradox of inequality and social class reveals itself in the following scenario that I share with students: "Garbage collectors and lawyers will go on strike tomorrow. In two weeks, whom will you miss the most and

49

why?"[1] Usually, the question stirs discussion of the ways in which culture legitimates some groups and tasks while it stigmatizes others. In this chapter, I draw upon a few sociological perspectives that are helpful in getting at a deeper understanding of inequality and poverty.

When people ask me how I managed to move out of poverty, I always get a lump in my throat. It is not because I am embarrassed to tell of my journey or because I want to forget that part of my past. Instead, I fear that people will think that I just decided to pull myself up by my bootstraps and, "Voilà!" I became middle class. Perhaps my greatest fear is that the person I speak with will turn to someone else in a similar situation and say, "All you have to do is want to make it and you can." Usually the question comes up abruptly: "Lori, why did *you* make it?" Often my response is, "Do you have eight hours to spare?" I do not wish to simplify such a complex issue with socially acceptable sound bites, such as, "Oh, I guess I just got lucky." Or worse yet, "Well, my parents were hard workers and they instilled a good work ethic in me, which I applied to educating myself."

The first few times I had this discussion, I found myself experiencing "survivor's guilt." I wondered why I had made it out while others were still burdened with acute poverty. I had a very strong gut feeling that I was normal. I do not mean for this to sound, as a social worker colleague would say, like "negative self talk." But I was like so many of the women I have met who are single parents for a myriad of reasons and are poor but did not choose to be.

I have come to believe that the routine of caring for and providing for our children the best we know how leads most of us to believe that what we see around us is both natural and normal. Most if not all of us tend to accept inequality in the abstract and try to adjust to it as best we can. I valued education as much as anyone, but circumstances got in the way time and time again. For a long while, furthering myself just never seemed plausible. But when the chance was offered, I gave it a shot. I have known many single parents who have had the same experience. We did not suddenly decide to sacrifice our time and energy for the sake of going to school; we were already working hard. We did not suddenly develop middle-class aspirations, and we were not somehow morally deficient. We *always* wanted more for our children and ourselves. I suppose what irritates me the most is the assumption that I somehow gained a new set of values that made me decide to move up and out of poverty.

Maybe my sense of being unfairly judged arises from one of the main misconceptions about poor people. That is, the poor are often assumed to be culturally different, and to possess different beliefs and values, from people in the middle class. The popular notion is that the poor create their own "brick wall" of values and beliefs that keeps them from rising above their situations. For example, poor people are thought to value immediate gratification, to be unable to plan for the long term. Under this view, sending poor single parents through college is essentially futile. Moreover, poor people are seen to have irresponsible patterns of behavior that are beyond what economic resources could cure.[2] Oscar Lewis, one of the early theorists identified with what has been called the "culture of poverty" perspective, wrote that young slum children were doomed to a life of poverty as young as age six or seven because they had already internalized the values of their subculture.[3]

It seems that discussions of poverty and inequality always and necessarily intersect with our understanding of culture. The implication of this way of thinking about the poor is that the culture of poverty will prevent them from taking advantage of any opportunities that might come their way. Further, a sense of obligation to community or a thirst for self-improvement are believed to be outside the range of values held by poor people. Accordingly, "low" culture is stubborn and resistant to change.

Lillian Rubin, a sociologist who has examined the contemporary worlds of poor and working class families, demonstrates how this logic is intellectually bankrupt, however popular it may be. She writes:

> These families reproduce themselves not because they are somehow deficient or their culture aberrant, but because there are no alternatives for most of their children. Indeed, it may be the singular triumph of this industrial society … that not only do we socialize people to their appropriate roles and stations, but that the process by which this occurs is so subtle that it is internalized and passed from parents to children by adults who honestly believe they are acting out of choices they have made in their own lifetime.[4]

Research has shown that most of the activities of the poor are necessarily limited to those which involve friends and relatives of their own socioeconomic status. Their exposure to alternative jobs or lifestyles is restricted, but this fact can hardly be equated with low aspirations. In fact, when the opportunity to go to college was first presented to me, I did not turn it down but instead replied, "Who me?"[5] In my world, there were few examples of poor women who were also college students. Sociologist Chaim

Waxman once wrote, "to adopt a line of conduct, one needs an image of the kind of world in which one is trying to act, a sense that one can read reasonably and accurately how one is doing."[6] For me and many of the single parents I met, a normal day in poverty is so challenging that notions such as self-improvement and contributing to the community become luxuries; being in survival mode, as Sarah so aptly put it, forces one to focus upon the demands of immediate subsistence. The point is not to argue for cultural injection—the instilling of the cultural values of one class into another—but instead to remind us that the cultural differences that are revealed through our habits, demeanor, and attitudes are in many ways shaped by social class.

Sociologist Pierre Bourdieu coined the term "cultural capital" to help explain how economic conditions play themselves out in our subjective worldviews through what he terms "habitus," a system of attitudes, likes, and dislikes that are shaped by our social class. In his study of French culture, Bourdieu (1984) distinguished between "aesthetic" taste and what he termed "taste of necessity," a phrase he used to describe working-class culture.[7] Culture, which is shaped by structural conditions, provides us with codes that guide our behavior. Accordingly, a "taste for necessity" implies an adaptation to and acceptance of the necessary. The practices of affluent members of society hold more social value than those of poor people, in part because those in positions of power determine what is valued.

Bourdieu is partially correct, in that structural conditions do indeed shape our culture and help to explain the *perceived* differences in values and tastes. However, it is dangerous to apply too broad a brush to those in poverty. Other sociologists have found that poor people are far from homogeneous. For example, in a study of homelessness in the United States, researchers found that 20 to 30 percent of these poorest of the poor can be classified as "new poor."[8] The perceived cultural distinctiveness or "taste for necessity" resides more in a patterned set of behaviors, routines, orientations, and lines of action, each of which are adaptive responses to the predicament of homelessness and poverty in everyday life.

The conditions of poverty are pragmatic: one action makes certain future actions more or less possible. For example, dropping out of high school after only a ninth-grade education made going to college almost a complete impossibility for me. On the other hand, having dropped out of school, I found that I aspired to jobs and circumstances that seemed plausible for someone with no credentials. Few of those offered any opportunity for advancement. Further, I socialized with others who shared my situation. I was not consciously thinking about the social factors that limited my opportunities; I simply felt unlucky.

Our lives are shaped by social patterns of which we are often unaware.[9] The popular notion that the poor suffer because they have a different value system than those who are not poor becomes a smokescreen or an intellectual detour. It is indeed fascinating to see how these well-established misperceptions are used, not only by middle and upper class Americans but by poor people as well. While we might know, individually, that things are not right, we often remain unaware of the structural sources of our discontent. The result is that, more often than not, we go along with the way things are and do not question the arrangements that determine our place in society. The notion that the individual, more than anything else, is responsible for his or her own situation influences our own self-assessment, which we know is very much contingent upon our social location in today's world.[10]

The widespread belief that some sort of antidote is needed for the poor in order to compensate for what they lack culturally is not simply misinformed; quite frankly it is insulting. Community involvement and self-sacrifice are hardly the exclusive domain of middle- and upper-class Americans.[11] In discussing these issues with my students, I suggest that we might better explain poverty if we focus on what is happening structurally to perpetuate the enormous inequalities in our culture. In other words, are there ways in which our institutions, such as the education system or the workplace, sustain inequality? Are some born with more advantages than others? Are there ways in which our gender and race, and even our geographic location, influence who gets what?

In fact, our social class is influenced by several factors. Some we have control over; others we do not. Sociologists assign social class by taking into account a person's income, occupation, and education. These three conditions, combined with race and gender, largely determine our location in the social arrangement of American society.

Sociologists also speak of various kinds of social mobility, or the extent to which our social class changes over time. *Intergenerational* mobility, for example, refers to the degree to which one is better or worse off than one's parents. *Intragenerational* mobility is the extent to which an individual experiences upward or downward mobility over a lifetime. *Structural* mobility is movement upward or down-ward according to large-scale changes in the occupational structure. This type of mobility affects large segments of the population. For example, in the 1980s and 1990s there was significant growth in upper-middle-class jobs, such as in the technology sector. Growth also occurred in the low-skill, low-wage sector, while mid-level jobs shrank in num-ber.[12] This polarized growth suggests a downward trend in structural mobility as the middle rung of the employment ladder narrows.[13]

What does this mean for single parents, especially sin-gle mothers? Quite simply, it means that without an edu-cation or substantial training, the best they can hope for are jobs at the bottom of the continuum paying poverty-level wages. These "secondary market" jobs, as they are called, do not offer adequate wages, health care and retire-ment benefits, job security, or opportunities for advance-ment.

Whether we experience upward or downward mobility depends upon several factors, but the most important of these is the circumstance of our birth. The socioeconomic status of the family into which we are born is the best pre-dictor of our own status as adults. Sociologists call this phe-nomenon *class inheritance*. The relationship is especially strong for affluent families, that .5 to 1 percent of the pop-ulation who belong to the upper class.[14] Outside of that small group, the connection is less clear. For the rest of us, our parents' socioeconomic status does, in fact, set in mo-tion a cycle that will affect our educational and occupa-tional opportunities. Still, our own educational achieve-ment becomes the best predictor of social mobility over the course of our lives (intragenerational mobility).

Sociologists tend to see education as a more important factor because the correlation is so simple—in general, the more education you have, the higher your income.[15] Overall, those with a four-year college degree can expect to earn $1,420,850 in a lifetime, compared to someone with a high school diploma at $820,870. For high school dropouts, expected lifetime earnings drop to $608,810.[16] While the link between education and income has always existed, some researchers argue that the relationship is more important than ever before as credentials become the badge of legitimacy.[17]

I agree with this assessment in so far as education has proven to be an effective means for reducing poverty, at least for individuals. But sociologists are correct to point out that it is hardly the universal answer for such a complex issue as poverty, and before I continue hailing the virtues of education, I must first acknowledge the many other factors that also account for women's social location. These include divorce; lack of child support, transportation, and affordable child care; their concentration in low-wage jobs; growth of the service sector and the decline in manufacturing; weakened unions; and continued discrimination in the workplace. While I address some of these issues in this chapter, it is also important to note that for me and the women with whom I spoke, pursuing higher education was a life-changing event that helped us gain greater control over our lives. The opportunities, resources, and cultural savvy our educations brought were essential in helping us to move out of poverty.[18] Other, less tangible things also came with our educations, like empowerment or the ability to cope with circumstances that once seemed beyond our control.[19]

Postsecondary education is viewed throughout American culture as necessary for gaining the credentials and skills that lead to advancement. Historically, educational credentials have been highly valued because they are so closely linked with social status and class advantage. Does this mean that formally educated individuals are necessarily smarter than those with informal experiences? Of course not. Intelligence is not the prerogative of middle-class individuals. Nevertheless, as sociologist Randall Collins (1971) argues, we live in a society that overemphasizes credentials. Thus, whether fairly or not, diplomas, degrees, and certificates serve as markers for potential employers, so much so that education affects one's chances to experience social class mobility.

However, not all social critics see additional education as the solution to inequality. Stanley Aronowitz (1997) argues that it has another function:

> The college or university degree may not guarantee a job, let alone a career, but it has become the premier sign that informs employers and other educational institutions that the candidate has endured a regimen that, on balance, assures their reliability ... the credential signifies the student's mobility aspirations, in particular their ability to endure a long journey toward an indefinite conclusion and their capacity to tolerate boredom.[20]

And although it remains the best indicator for mobility today, post-secondary education does not guarantee a level playing field. In other words, earning a college degree does not fully erase the effects of social class, race, and gender. As Table 4.1 reveals, educational attainment influences incomes significantly. Still, women and minorities earn much

Table 4.1   U.S. Mean Annual Income by Educational Level
Completed, 1998 (dollars)

Mean Income	No High School Diploma	High School Graduate	Some College	Bachelor's Degree	Professional Degree
All persons	16,124	22,895	24,804	40,478	95,148
Males	19,575	28,307	31,268	50,056	109,206
Females	10,725	16,906	18,104	30,119	62,113
All whites	16,596	23,618	25,442	41,439	97,488
All blacks	13,185	18,980	22,105	32,062	51,004
All Hispanics	15,069	19,558	20,825	33,465	*

*Base figure too small to calculate.

Source: U.S. Bureau of the Census. 1998. *Current Population Reports,* P20-513. Washington, D.C.: U.S. Government Printing Office.

less than their white male counterparts with the same level of education.

Class

Colleges and universities, especially private ones, remain elite institutions that act in many ways to perpetuate class divisions. For this reason, it is useful to begin with social class, a primary determinant of educational opportunity. Wealth, as I mentioned earlier, is what allows for the transfer of opportunities from one generation to the next, and is thus a very strong predictor of who goes to college. To illustrate, from 1975 to 1994, high school students from upper- and upper-middle-class families were far more likely than other students to enroll in college and even more likely to go beyond the bachelor's degree into professional and graduate schools.

The more affluent a student's family, the greater the likelihood that he or she will be accepted into an Ivy

League school.[21] A study that followed the enrollments of eighteen- and nineteen-year-old high school graduates from the poorest and the richest fifths of American families found that while only 27 percent of the poor went on to college, 60 percent of those from affluent families enrolled.[22]

Higher education is not cheap. Soaring costs in recent decades have made it increasingly difficult for students from low-income families to remain in school.[23] Single parents, many of whom have to work full-time while attending college, are finding it harder to maintain their financial aid, academic standing, and job responsibilities simultaneously. The result has been a decrease in college enrollment among low-income students. I will introduce some individuals who are struggling with these issues in the next chapter.

Increasing costs are only one of the obstacles low-income students must contend with. Another is that college classrooms are not always a supportive environment. There is ample evidence of bias in the areas of class, race, and gender, even at the college level. Unfortunately, one's demeanor and the expression of values that indicate one's social class are still used by professors, not necessarily consciously, to weed out those perceived not to belong.[24] Students from affluent families often come with extra advantages, such as familiarity with aspects of culture that are highly valued in a college setting (e.g., music, art, literature).

These divisions do not begin in college, they just continue there. Social class bias is present in both elementary and secondary education.[25] In fact, at these levels, education has been shown to prepare students not according to their abilities but according to their social class. Schools are not the same everywhere, regardless of how democratic we may think they have become. Teachers develop ideas of what roles groups of students will assume when they go into the world of work and prepare them according to what they understand to be their parents' social class. Children from affluent families are better prepared through role modeling, school funding, personnel, better facilities, exposure, and resources, than children from lower-income families.[26] Kids in the poorest school districts often have the highest student–teacher ratios, the least technology, smaller libraries, fewer opportunities for tutors, and less parental supervision (since parents are often working after school hours). Adding to the odds facing poor children, teachers are shown to have higher expectations for children from affluent families throughout the schooling process.[27]

Educational tracking, a widely used practice, has proven most effective in channeling students into blue-collar and white-collar occupations according to their social class origins.[28] And although the stated purpose of tracking is to permit students to pursue studies that are the best fit for their innate abilities, research bears out this class-oriented aspect of tracking.[29] Hence, working class kids are being prepared for low-wage, marginal work, while middle-class kids are put on the college track. Those who attend college are already a minority, with 81.6 percent of Americans holding a high school diploma but only 23 percent holding a college degree. And as the following quotes demonstrate, social class greatly influences who goes to college, regardless of ability:

> Among high intelligence high school students, 91% [of higher-class students] attend college compared to 40% of

highly intelligent lower-class students. Conversely, 58% of students with low intelligence but higher-class backgrounds attend college compared to 9% of low intelligence, lower-class high school students. No matter what their intelligence, 84% of students from higher-class backgrounds go to college but only 21% from lower-class families do so. . . .[30]

College attendance continues to be important, of course, even if a person does not acquire skills needed for the job market. Those who finish college have a nearly 50% occupational advantage over those who do not.[31]

Race

Race and ethnicity remain important factors influencing social mobility in the United States. Being born white or "European American" does not guarantee wealth, power, and prestige, but it does mean that race will not hamper one's social mobility. In other words, being white in our society will not serve as a barrier.[32] The more visible one's minority status, the more significant race and ethnicity become, even to being the overriding determinant of one's social location.

Jonathan Kozol's book *Savage Inequalities* (1991) documents the inequities between poor and wealthy school districts and makes the argument that poor and minority students receive a diluted education, in part because of the differences between the districts in spending for public education, differences that are both directly and indirectly related to academic achievement.[33]

Other research has shown that African American and Hispanic students are singled out at a much higher rate for "special education" classes, resulting in labeling that may lead to a self-fulfilling prophecy.[34] Thus, according to many

Table 4.2 Educational Attainment by Race and Ethnic Origin, 1970–1998 (percentage in U.S. completing four or more years of college)

Year	Total	White	Black	Asian and Pacific Islander	Hispanic*
1970	10.7	11.3	4.4	NA	4.5
1975	13.9	14.5	6.4	NA	NA
1980	16.2	17.1	8.4	NA	7.6
1985	19.4	20.0	11.1	NA	8.5
1990	21.3	22.0	11.3	39.9	9.2
1995	23.0	24.0	13.2	NA	9.3
1997	23.9	24.6	13.3	42.2	10.3
1998	14.4	25.0	14.7	NA	11.0

*"Hispanic" includes Americans of Mexican, Puerto Rican, and Cuban origin.

Source: U.S. Bureau of the Census. 1999. U.S. Census Population, U.S. Summary, PC80-1-C1, and Current Population reports. *Statistical Abstract of the United States: 1999.* Washington, D.C.: U.S. Government Printing Office.

sociologists, primary, secondary, and even post-secondary education acts as a device that sorts students along the lines of class and race.[35]

As I stated earlier, college graduates represent about 25 percent of the U.S. population, but there are stark differences in the rate of completion among different racial and ethnic groups, as Table 4.2 shows. In 1997, for example, almost 25 percent of whites were college graduates while 42 percent of Asian Americans were. Although graduation rates among African Americans have risen since 1970, they remain far lower than those of whites and Asian Americans. Among Hispanics the graduation rates increased somewhat less than for blacks, from 4.5 percent in the 1970s to 11 percent in 1998.[36] Not shown are Native Americans, who have the lowest rate at 0.8 percent. And because education is a key factor in determining an individual's life chances, the differences have important consequences.

Today, 26 percent of African Americans and 25.6 percent of American Hispanics live in poverty. For Native Americans, the figure soars to almost 50 percent. Compare that to 10.5 percent of whites living in poverty.[37] Moreover, in female-headed households, the figures rise to 40.8 percent for African Americans, 43.7 percent for Hispanics, and 24.9 percent for whites. In 1995 the median annual household income for whites was $37,178, as compared to $22,860 for blacks and $22,393 for Latinos. Moreover, if we look for a moment at wealth or our net worth (assets minus debts), we are faced with an even starker reality.

In 1993 white households had an average net worth of $45,740, compared to $4,418 for black households.[38] These figures are especially telling because it is wealth that allows us to go to college, hire tutors, obtain reliable transportation, make payments on a house, or pay for emergencies. Yet for entire groups in this country, decent health care and housing, a high-quality education, and a living wage are but a dream. Almost half of the adult poor are employed (48 percent), and the working poor (those who earn between 125 and 150 percent of the poverty level) now constitute 25 percent of all workers. Young adults are especially affected. Nearly half of all women and over one-third of men between the ages of 18 and 24 belong to the working poor.[39] When we acknowledge this reality, we are forced to admit that poverty and race are directly related to educational attainment. I turn next to gender, an equally important influence on social mobility.

Gender

Women in Arkansas are economically and socially disadvantaged in a number of ways relative to women in other states. For example, their average annual earnings ($14,000) fall far below the national median for all full-time workers ($18,778). The Institute for Women's Policy Research in Washington, D.C., ranked women in the fifty states and the District of Columbia on measures of education, poverty, and occupational status. Arkansas ranked fiftieth in the category of education (for the percentage having completed four or more years of college), forty-ninth for the numbers living in poverty, and forty-eighth in the category of occupational status (that is, the percentage of women employed in managerial or professional occupations). Given these dismal statistics, the personal journeys completed by many of the women in this book become even more remarkable.

As we consider how gender influences one's life chances, there is both good news and bad news for women. The good news is that from 1960 to 1995, women went from being outnumbered two to one by their male counterparts to being the majority of students enrolled in college.[40] The bad news is that women are far less likely than male students to earn postgraduate degrees, while they are likely to need more education than their male counterparts in order to compete successfully for top positions.[41] Situational factors, such as divorce, family obligations, child care costs, and time constraints, keep single parents far underrepresented at both the undergraduate and graduate levels in comparison to their single and married women counterparts.

Despite the fact that more women are attending college, the classroom has not proven overly friendly to females. Research has shown that in secondary schools male students are called upon more often than females and receive more attention and encouragement from teachers. This trend prevails in college classrooms as well,[42] where female students are recognized less frequently than males, are more often interrupted or ignored when they do speak, and where their comments are more often devalued by professors and by their male peers.[43]

For single mothers who do not obtain a college degree, the battle for upward mobility is, in many ways, already lost. But even those who complete their degree find that the workplace presents another challenge. Unfortunately, education does not guarantee occupational status or pay equity. This is especially so for women and people of color, given that both need more education than men to compete for the same jobs.[44]

The topics that sociologists choose to study are influenced by their own cultural backgrounds as well as by historical context. Women and minorities were underrepresented in the profession until the 1960s, but as they entered the profession in increasing numbers, race and gender became recognized as legitimate subjects of study. For example, little research focused on women and work because of the widespread assumption that women were supplemental income earners at best. For example, in the 1940s, sociologist Talcott Parsons examined the roles and status of men and women. He applied what sociologists call a functionalist perspective to understand the interrelated components of social systems—in this case, the family. Men, he found, performed instrumental tasks and had visible roles as breadwinners, whereas women's statuses were determined by those of their husbands and their roles were expressive, with tasks defined in terms of family maintenance and child rearing. He wrote, "The most fundamental basis of the family's status is the occupational status of the husband and father." Women's status, he continued, is "that of her husband's wife, the mother of his children and traditionally the person responsible for a complex of activities in the management of the household, care of children, etc."[45]

Today Americans understand that women are often forced to work outside the home, even while they may continue to carry out traditional roles within the family. Single mothers typically have no choice but to juggle breadwinner and family roles. Imagine, then, the stress for single mothers in a work culture that still holds to outdated notions of family and still views women as supplemental income earners and as primary caregivers for children. A 1996 U.S. survey found that the workplace is still unsupportive of families. One-third of working parents (both mothers and fathers) feel that they still have to choose between advancement in their jobs and taking time to care for their families. And when they do choose the latter, they are looked upon unfavorably.[46]

Workplace norms impose much heavier demands upon single parents than on two-parent families. This is especially true for single mothers, given the discrepancy in their earnings compared to those of men. The pressure for full participation in both spheres, work and home, takes a toll emotionally, mentally, and physically. Policy makers, by and large, still ignore this misunderstood phenomenon when it comes to single mothers, especially those who are transitioning from welfare to work. Longer transition periods, extended health coverage, and child care would aid single mothers as they attempt to gain a foothold in the workplace. Increased sensitivity and allowance for family leave are essential for those households with only one caregiver.

Gender disparities occur in the labor market at several levels, and gender-segregated workplaces account for a significant part. Today women remain highly concentrated in occupations such as secretarial work, retail sales, food preparation, teaching, nursing, cashiering, and bookkeeping. While these are worthy occupations, the fact that they have been historically female means that they pay less than traditionally male occupations requiring the same level of education and training. Even within these predominantly female occupations, male employees experience more mobility, although the larger the proportion of women in an occupation, the lower are the wages both women and men earn. Indeed, not only are men singled out for promotions to higher-level positions in traditionally female occupations (most school principals are male, for example), but when they do not seek promotion, they are often stigmatized for not taking a "male" approach to their work.[47] In the end, not only are men and women segregated into different jobs, those differences are unequal.

In almost all occupations, the most powerful positions are reserved for male employees. Women supervise fewer subordinates than their male counterparts, have less authority and fewer decision-making opportunities, and less control over financial resources.[48] In addition, women remain significantly underrepresented at the top levels of major U.S. corporations. Of almost thirteen thousand corporate officers in Fortune 500 companies in 1996, only 10 percent were women.[49] And while women have steadily gained access to professional and managerial positions, the best-paying and most influential of these positions are still reserved for men. For example, women today constitute about 26 percent of all lawyers but they represent only about 2 percent of partners in major law firms.[50]

Consequently, while education remains crucial—providing the necessary credentials to compete in the job market—pay disparity is equally important. For example, in 1992 women with college degrees earned only $2,000 more than white men with only a high school diploma.[51] When education is held constant, women earn less than men in all categories. For example, among males and females with a bachelor's degree, women earn only 71 percent of what males earn. Among those with master's degrees, the disparity narrows slightly, to 73 percent, but then widens to 63 percent for those with professional degrees. Women who hold doctorates earn about 74 percent of men in the same category.

Sociologists disagree over the causes of these differences. One explanation is the "glass ceiling" phenomenon. The metaphor is used to describe organizational cultures in which there is room for advancement, but where women rarely reach the top. This may be because women are also excluded from the core positions that would allow the networking necessary for advancement. Another factor may be that women have few female role models and suffer from a lack of mentoring.

A more popular explanation has to do with the popular notion of individualism I discussed in Chapter 3. For example, human-capital theorists have long argued that the market is fair and that women do less well than men because they invest less in their jobs. Women are faulted for not approaching their careers as men do. They are said to possess traits that do not serve them well in the workplace—everything from passive and submissive personalities, to lack of relevant education and work experience.

Because women typically have more family responsibilities than men, they are perceived to be less committed to their careers. They are believed to devote less time to their training and skill development, and they average less work experience than men. There is some truth in all these points, but it is important to remember the structural conditions that make it difficult for women to match men's career patterns.

Though women are more likely to finish high school than men, they are less likely to earn advanced degrees beyond the Bachelors. Training in the workplace has been historically sex stereotyped. Employers have invested less in on-the-job training for females than males. In many cases, women have historically been expected to receive their training and education elsewhere, because employers perceived them as less committed, less willing to invest long-term in their jobs, and more likely to be absent from their jobs to care for family. Such perceptions served to justify lower investment in female employees. Indeed, they have been partially correct in that women do spend less time in the work place overall. They have intermittent work patterns compared to their male counterparts as the result of such factors as child birth and parental and child caregiving. Having some historical accuracy, these assumptions become institutionalized and limit future opportunities for men and women before they can choose. Again, single mothers are caught in the crossfire; they need the wages and consequent human capital investment from their employers but they are also the only caregiver. These kinds of differences in schooling and training, as well as job experience, have contributed to women's overall lower status in the workplace.[52]

It is estimated that about one half of the difference in pay between males and females is due, in part, to voluntary segregation. Women are more likely to seek out those jobs that fit traditional "female" stereotypes. What remains most perplexing today is the fact that traditionally female occupations are still devalued. The higher the wages in a particular job setting, the fewer females employed. Likewise, the higher the number of women in a particular occupation, the lower the overall wages. While women are socialized to accept traditionally female jobs, men are socialized to seek out positions of authority, higher pay, and promotional opportunities, and to enforce these expectations in the workplace. Research has shown this to be the case for decades. But as a society we have acknowledged the changing structure of families. We recognize the need for dual income earning families. We encourage fathers to take more active roles in caregiving. We praise "stay at home" dads. We realize that many women no longer work for "pin" money but that their incomes are essential to their family's survival. We have admitted to ourselves as a society that many children will grow up in single parent households (most with single mothers). Hence, it is not clear why these status differences remain in place today.

Men are still often viewed as the family breadwinner, a stereotype that no longer fits today's economic realities and certainly is not relevant for single mothers. Today, while more than half of all adult women work, their incomes are still seen as supplemental. Women's continuing responsibilities for child care and domestic work may contribute to this perception, and employers may particularly see single parents as less committed to their careers than other employees. An alternative would be to view them as breadwinners. There may be no greater loyalty than that of a single parent to an employer who understands the nature of family responsibilities but is willing to look long term at the contributions of that individual.

5 Chance and Choice

The full range of changes that education brings about are hard to capture in quantifiable ways, but they are monumental for those of us who have experienced them. I remember when my first-semester grades arrived in the mail in December 1984. Walking back from the mailbox, I felt a jolt in the pit of my stomach as I opened the envelope to find I had made an A in each one of my courses. I drove to a phone booth and called my mother to tell her. She was silent for a moment. When she finally spoke, her voice cracked and she was crying. "I am so proud of you," she said. "I am just so proud of you." Even as I write about this experience many years later, I can return to that moment, those feelings, and her words of encouragement.

But not everyone has the encouragement or the necessary safety net of supportive family members and friends. And while there are far more success stories than failures among scholarship recipients, not everyone succeeds. Some slip through the safety net and land hard. Those who drop out often do so because they began their studies at a significant disadvantage, with unresolved problems that only magnify and grow.

One woman, in particular, affirmed for me that the reasons for not finishing school can be complex. Jonetta is twenty-three years old and she has two children. "I had my kids young," she laughs, "but I can't keep up with them now." Toby, the youngest, is four years old. He runs through the aisles in Wal-Mart as Jonetta and I talk in the McDonald's snack bar toward the back of the store. Joseph, the oldest at six, is in school. Jonetta describes him as her "little man" of the house: "He keeps a close eye on Toby when I'm too tired to deal with him."

Jonetta received two single parent scholarships before she had to quit school. She never actually said whether her TEA assistance ran out and she was forced to work, or whether she quit school voluntarily. "Yeah, I liked it [going to school]," she begins, "but I don't see myself doing it again. I didn't do too good," she adds. She resisted the temptation to take out student loans for fear of having to drop out: "Then I'll be stuck with student loans on top of everything else." Jonetta had a clear understanding of the cost of education and feared getting in over her head. She has known individuals who completed their education and are now in debt for student loans that they are unable to repay with their current earnings.

Nervous and somewhat pessimistic about her future, Jonetta does not expect to return to school, although she might reconsider "once both kids are in school." She earns just enough from her job with Wal-Mart to keep her ineligible for any type of assistance. Moreover, when her former boyfriend pays child support, her income is enough to keep her family afloat. "He's been pretty good for the last six or seven months," she claims. When asked to imagine her life ten years from now, Jonetta pauses and takes a deep breath. "I imagine I'll still be here," she says. "Would that be so bad?" I asked. She smiles and responds, "Well, it wasn't what I had in mind."

Felt ambivalence is the best way to describe Jonetta's situation. She is intelligent and personable, and she may be able to advance in her job. But intelligence and personality will likely not be enough to help Jonetta in the long term, given the structural constraints that she is likely to face without credentials and an education. Jonetta will have a difficult time advancing in her work if she has to compete with someone with a college degree.

A different host of reasons caused Julie, the oldest single mother I interviewed, to suspend her schooling. When Julie's ex-husband and his new wife began expecting their first child, she knew the child-support payments would be even slower and more sporadic than they already were. "Now my former husband had a stepdaughter, one of his children living with him, and one on the way. I knew the child support would be even less regular. Guess what," she says, "I was right." Today the child support has "dried up," as she puts it. Her income is just over $20,000 per year, but her nineteen-year-old son does not have health insurance, and as Julie describes it, "Sometimes it costs more than when I had him at home."

Julie's first husband did not want her to work or attend school, and during her second marriage, she worked to help her husband finish a degree in agricultural business. After that marriage ended, Julie was able to attend school part-time and work part-time as a receptionist and accounting clerk at a local insurance agency. But when the child support began to falter, she needed to increase her hours. Her full-time job brought her wages up to more than 150 percent above poverty, too high to qualify for the single parent scholarship. But this was not why she chose to leave school. As she explains, "I just could not have any time left for mothering and parenting at all while working full-time too. It was at that point that I dropped out of school."

Julie's situation is similar to that of other single mothers, especially those without the safety net of family and friends. However, unlike most of the others, she plans to return to school at some point, perhaps after her youngest child leaves home. For her, college was a good experience but one that "came a little too early." Perhaps Julie seems like an anomaly because she remains hopeful. I would have expected her to be less enthusiastic about returning to school at forty-three years of age. Research has shown that one barrier to continuing education is the belief that one is too old.[1] However, Julie expects that soon none of her children will be left at home. Consequently, it may be easier for her to envision being a student than it is for younger mothers with school-age children to support. She would like to pursue a degree in counseling and hopes someday to specialize in art therapy. Speaking to Julie was uplifting, mostly because her self-esteem appeared to have survived her many struggles. Certainly, this was not the case for many of the women who dropped out.

Andrea is twenty-one years old and, like Jonetta, is more typical of the women who dropped out. She has a nine-month-old child. While the father of her child is in the same town, he lives with his new girlfriend. Tears flow freely as Andrea describes her situation. She lives with her parents but the conditions are not satisfactory. Andrea's mother and stepfather are alcoholics, and she believes her situation is worse now than when she lived in public housing. "They don't want me here but I don't have any place to go. I'm stuck."

Andrea received three support payments, but her ex-boyfriend recently declared that he is not the father of her child. She is currently struggling to decide whether to pursue testing for paternity. She realizes that in order to receive assistance and move out of her parents' house, she will have to agree to proceed with it, but so far fear of angering her ex-boyfriend has immobilized her and kept her from having the test done.

Andrea received only one scholarship before she chose to drop out of school. The decision to quit was not connected to eligibility. Instead, it was readily apparent that she lacked confidence in herself. "I would be the first in our family if I'd went," she tells me with a near smile. But Andrea receives little emotional support or encouragement to continue her education and appears, at present, to be resigned to "flipping burgers."

Like so many other young women, Andrea had visions of a bright future with her boyfriend, but when she became pregnant the relationship soured almost immediately. Andrea may someday return to school and apply for the scholarship. She is still young and may have experiences that lead her back to college. However, her social network will have to widen and her self-esteem will need to improve greatly to enhance her chances of success.

What saddens me most about Andrea and so many single mothers that I have known, myself included, is that because they have low self-esteem they fear that they will not be able to make choices down the road that will lead to further advancement. The catch-22 is that this keeps them from getting started. What I found, and others have confirmed this, is that getting started may require consciously "acting as if" one can succeed, regardless of how fearful we may be.

A stronger social network might empower Andrea and strengthen the self-esteem that would help carry her through the struggles she faces. For me this was my family, who insisted I try and encouraged me not to give up. There was also the important symbolism of a scholarship and what that meant to me, namely that others thought I could succeed. But without enough of these resources, Andrea may indeed be "stuck."

Those former scholarship recipients who completed school appear to have fared much better overall. Perhaps this is because for Americans without a high-school diploma, the chances of living in poverty are one in four. For those with at least four years of high school, it drops to nearly one in ten, and for Americans with a four-year college degree or more, the poverty rate drops to a dramatic 2 percent.[2] In 1996 female high school graduates averaged annual earnings of $14,995, compared to $30,538 for those with a bachelor's degree or more.[3] These figures call to mind the pithy bumper sticker, "If you think education is expensive, try ignorance." But education means much more for the families than just income potential.

Indeed, for many single mothers, the benefits far outweighed the costs. Obtaining an education does far more than simply increase household income, which by itself would be reward enough. But education also provides intangible benefits. It is as if higher education serves as a catalyst for life-long change. Single mothers often begin with a myriad of obstacles. We bring with us the baggage of low self-esteem, uncertainty, fear of failure, and a desire to hide our inadequacies. We exit with a comprehensive set of tools that can empower us and our children as well.

The results varied, but the women interviewed in this study shared emotionally charged accounts of how education changed their lives, gave them confidence, enhanced their self-esteem and personal well-being, and changed their expectations not only for themselves but for their children. The positive effects of education cannot be denied for this group of women. Obviously, obtaining an education may not result in gainful employment for everyone, but it appears to provide the foundation for change that will sustain many of these women.

The pursuit of an education involves confidence building at each phase of one's academic career, from the first excellent grade on a test or paper to the diploma received at graduation. A good example is Regina, an occupational therapist who has finally entered the nurturing profession she desired to pursue and now sets her own hours and is able to travel. While the change is most obvious for Regina, it has affected her children in important ways as well. Now, she says, "we can buy almost anything we want. We have a wonderful, large home. I have a nice car. I have a fine job where I'm well respected." She continues, "They [the children] have nicer clothes. When my oldest child was growing up, she owned one pair of shoes at a time. That's what I could afford. Things have changed tremendously. . . . When my firstborn was a kid, things like college didn't even enter my mind." Now, not only does Regina fully expect her own children to continue their educations, she cannot imagine what life would be like today had she not gone to college.

Sandi, like Regina, credits her education with opening new possibilities. She explained that getting good grades, earning credits, feeling her self-confidence increase, and earning her diploma collectively gave her a new world-view. "I dream big now. I never say 'never' because if I can do this, I can reach for the stars."

Roweena had just left an abusive relationship when she returned to school. When asked about her children, she explained, "I think showing them that you can move on in-stead of dwell on it—they're seeing me be a stronger per-son. School built my self-esteem, showing me that I proved I could finish and work hard at it even though I was down and at a time where I thought I wouldn't go anywhere." Both her children are still young, but Roweena now has a secure job as an administrative assistant for an insurance company. "My main concern," she says, "is to get them the education they need to help them along. I want to let them know there are better things out there."

Delta was thirty when her son was born. She has only one child, and he has always seen her working hard, even before she returned to college. "There are certain things I would like to see him do," she says. "And of course, he's going to chart his own course, but I think setting a good example is the best a parent can do and hope and pray for the best."

The more economic resources parents have, the greater are the opportunities available to their children. The higher one's income, the greater one's likelihood of living in a neighborhood with access to high-quality public and pri-vate schooling, and the more likely it is that one's children will attend college. As the incomes of these women in-crease, so too do the cultural resources available to their children, such as exposure to magazines, books, travel, cultural diversity, computers, the Internet, tutors, and enriching extracurricular activities.

Greater social ease also comes with education.[4] As these women become more empowered and gain more control over their lives, they can advocate both for their children and for themselves in ways that were not possible before. They feel more comfortable and confident with their children's teachers and school principals.[5] They become part of the implied partnership between parents and educators that is essential to ensuring their children's academic success. The more educated the parent, the more likely she is to read to her children, help with their homework, instill successful study habits, and to possess cultural knowledge that is consistent with the cultural expectations of educators.[6] Thus, while the women (many of them first-generation college graduates) have certainly benefited by obtaining their educations, their children will be beneficiaries as well.

The educational gains flow from one generation to the next as these women develop increased self-efficacy. Children witness their mothers' effective coping strategies and the powerful modeling for success. Over time, they benefit by acquiring a particular orientation to the world that encompasses knowledge of those components of culture that hold more social value. The result is an ability to be savvy in a world that judges us upon our academic and cultural competence. As I discussed in Chapter 4, research has confirmed that students with the most "cultural capital" are also the ones who tend to obtain the highest levels of education and get the higher-status jobs.[7]

Penny, a first-generation college graduate, explained that one of her daughters had chosen not to attend college at present, but "She knows that she can go back later." No doubt this is a lesson both daughters have learned from Penny, who graduated with a bachelor's degree in business administration at forty years of age. I asked Penny how getting a college degree had affected her. "For one thing," she said, "I thought I was a fairly good person beforehand, but college really rounds a person out. It's a big difference. It widens your viewpoint and keeps you from being, well, quite so narrow." She attributes her new "craving" for diverse experiences to having gone to college.

As Penny described it, she and her daughters were almost equally involved in college activities, especially something called the "hospitality society." "I was very involved and was president of it, and they [her daughters] got involved with a lot of our projects. They even got temporary memberships and awards for their help."

Anna believes that her education has greatly impacted her daughter's understanding about school. "I think it's been very productive. We went from a situation where we really didn't have a whole lot, and I wanted her to understand the value of what it means to have an education and then to have an occupation that can be productive. I've been able to provide a lot better for her since my accomplishments. . . . I've always set out for her to get an education and to proceed with it as far as she would like to take it. It's not an issue that I would ever force on her." But Anna is confident that she has been a model for her daughter, who says she wants to be a nurse, the same profession her mother has chosen.

Latonya has twin boys, aged eleven. She is so convinced that education can change lives that she cannot imagine her sons not continuing their educations after high school:

"I had made up my mind a long time ago that when I discussed college with them it wasn't going to be 'if,' it was going to be 'when.' *When* you go to college, not *if* you go to college."

Debbie's daughter has a learning disability that has just been diagnosed. She believes her own education has helped her to face this challenge. "I think me going on through school is helping her. . . . It helped me be a better person with my self-esteem so I know where to help [her daughter] more. So she doesn't fall in my trap. 'Cause when you have someone there say, 'Oh, you can do it' or 'I'll support you,' it helps."

Jackie raised four children. After thirteen years of marriage, she left Austin, Texas, and brought her children to Arkansas to be closer to her parents. After a few years of odd jobs, she returned to school part-time. "Getting that first A was a jump start," she explains. "It was just, 'I can do it! I can achieve this!' I retained a 4.0 grade point [average] for a long time. I finally got one B, but it was such an ego builder to go out there and start achieving in academia. It really helped." When I asked Jackie how her education had affected her children, she responded, "You know how your kids are. They think you're stupid. But when I went back to college, they saw that mom can do it and they can too."

Jackie's response to the scholarship was similar to others I heard. She remembers her first interview with the scholarship board. "I was so nervous the first time," she recalls. "But it made me feel special." I shared with Jackie my own reaction to receiving the scholarship, and she added, "Yeah, they believe in you when nobody else does."

Karen explained that her education has benefited her children "profoundly." She struggled over how much she should expose her children to the hard work of studying. "I found a compromise. I studied during the weekdays after 8:00 P.M. and studied on the weekends in front of them. Rick [her son] has recently said that he's going for his Ph.D. Before, they didn't have a concept of bachelor's or master's or anything. But he's going for a Ph.D., he says."

Karen also was quick to speak of the safety net provided by her parents. "My parents were there for me too. Especially my mom. I don't think I could have done it without their moral support. They call and ask about the kids, and they tell me how proud they are of me in front of them. I think that helps." I asked Karen if she felt the same about the scholarship staff. She agreed and added, "That's exactly how it feels, like an extended support group."

These comments suggest that while the generational effect of an education may be subtle, it is extremely important. As their children grow into adulthood, they will find that continuing their education is plausible because they have been exposed to the changing realities of their own parents' lives. There is hope in the voices of these women as they look toward their children's futures.

For those who did not finish their degrees, the reasons were complex and not always clear. While I could not develop a clear profile of a "dropout," there did seem to be evidence that when needs are not met (such as for adequate child support, affordable child care, reliable transportation, adequate time for parenting, and emotional support), a woman's chances of staying in school are reduced. And while these women are now working for wages, they did not demonstrate any marked improvement in their standard of living, beyond meeting the most basic needs. A week of work missed to care for a sick child or a serious transportation problem could put any one of them at risk, forcing them to start again from scratch. Next, I outline some strategies for initiating a scholarship fund and suggest policy changes that can help reduce poverty among struggling single parent families.

6 Starting a Single Parent Scholarship Program

Ingredients for Success

Nonprofit organizations have been forced to step up their efforts as federal and state governments continue to reduce their support for social programs of various kinds. In the past decade, contributions from individuals, foundations, and corporations have constituted a significant portion of revenue for nonprofits, with some estimates as high as one-fifth of their total income.[1] The growing demand for services, however, means heightened competition for funds among the more than one million nonprofits in the United States formed to meet various social needs.

Nonprofits differ in the extent to which they rely on grants or gifts. Regardless of the resources available, fundraising is always key. This is especially the case for the nonprofits that rely more on private giving and less on grants. A clear understanding of both the social problem and the proposed community solution are a must for organizations that have formed in response to community needs.

This chapter is addressed to readers interested in starting their own scholarship fund. I review some important steps that should be taken to get an organization on its feet, beginning with a brief history of the Arkansas Single Parent

Scholarship Fund. Because of its incredible success, readers may want to use it as a template for their own scholarship program.

A Brief History

In 1983 Ralph Nesson, the current director of the ASPSF, was serving as the community development specialist for the Economic Opportunity Agency of Washington County, in northwest Arkansas. The mission of that organization was to develop antipoverty strategies through partnerships with governmental and non-governmental agencies. At the request of the EOA's state funding agency, a needs survey was conducted. In addition to obtaining opinions on antipoverty strategies, it aimed to consider future directions and projects. About fifteen hundred county residents were interviewed in the survey.

The philosophy for what would become the Single Parent Scholarship Fund emerged from the overwhelming response to the survey. It was "plain common sense," Ralph explained. The strongest need was to "educate and train poor folks so they [would] be able to get out of poverty." In fact, this response was repeated so often and in so many settings that it helped Ralph to identify his next step: to talk directly with poor people and educators about existing education and training programs and to see how EOA might support these efforts.

Ralph then teamed up with Marjorie Marugg-Wolfe, the coordinator of a federally funded program within the Northwest Arkansas Vocational-Technical Institute called Single Parents and Homemakers in Transition. Both Ralph and Marjorie had been striving individually to make lives better for single parents. Together they began discussions with others in the community.

First located in the small EOA office, the Washington County Single Parent Scholarship Fund began awarding scholarships of $300 per semester. The scholarships were funded by a group of local citizens, who donated both money and time to help establish the fund. They were a "roll up your sleeves" advisory board but not a legal entity, Ralph recalls.

In January 1984 the Scholarship Fund began functioning under the legal umbrella of EOA in Washington County and the Office of Human Concern in Benton County, where it remained until 1992. One of the program's first hurdles was to get past the catch-22 enforced by the Food Stamp Program as administered by the Arkansas Department of Human Services. It required that all non-governmental financial aid to food-stamp recipients be reported as income and deducted from their monthly allotments. Realizing that enforcement of this guideline would severely limit the effectiveness of their efforts, Ralph and Marjorie met with the DHS officials and learned of the "vendor system." The Scholarship Fund could forward scholarship awards directly to vendors, such as child care providers, repair shops, and bookstores, allowing clients to avoid the loss of much-needed food stamps.

With the distribution of the first round of scholarships, the system was in place to raise money for each successive semester. The intent was to minimize state and federal grant support by going to the local community: small businesses, corporations, and individual donors. This method proved both efficient and rewarding. Not only could the donors and the local advisory board cut through the red tape by having say over the spending, but they could get to know the people they were assisting, the true "heart" of the project.

Single parents applied for scholarships up to three times per year (for the fall, spring, and summer semesters). The application requested information on their income, family status, and education. Each applicant was also asked to submit an essay outlining his or her goals and explaining how the scholarship would be used to further them. Next they attended an interview with a few of the board members and the program director.

This meeting was informal. Applicants could bring their children if child care was not available, and they met with the program administrators around a table where refreshments were served. The board members would introduce themselves, and then Ralph Nesson would ask how the previous semester had gone. He also wanted to know whether the applicants were aware of the programs in place that could supplement the scholarship assistance, such as housing subsidies, food stamps, and student-loan programs. He concluded by asking whether applicants had any questions for the board or for him. A fairly painless task for all involved, the interview provided a symbolic link between recipient and donor that would help to define the nature of the project.

ASPSF Today

This system, with few modifications, continues to operate today. Since the fund's beginning, more than $2.5 million have been awarded to over fifty-eight hundred scholarship recipients. As of 2000, 85 percent of the recipients had either graduated or were still in school. More importantly, 70 percent of graduates are earning wages that lift them above poverty.[2]

Criteria for scholarship eligibility remain similar to those established early on in Washington County. Although the policies of each county affiliate vary according to the preferences of local boards of directors, some general guidelines are used by all the affiliates. Applicants are considered if they earn low to moderate incomes (180 to 185 percent of the poverty threshold), are residents of the county in which the application is submitted, are the custodial parent of at least one child under the age of eighteen, and are already enrolled in a career-directed post-secondary course of study leading to a diploma, degree, or license.[3] As mentioned in the Preface, while single fathers are eligible to apply, over 99 percent of the applicants have been women.

Enrollment at an accredited institution of higher education is not an ASPSF requirement, although the vast majority of scholarships are used for vocational/technical training or to attend a community college or university. Each affiliate awards scholarships according to the post-secondary resources available in their respective locations. In the past scholarships have also been given to students in such non-academic programs as aviation technology, massage therapy, and cosmetology. Some counties are more flexible than others, depending upon the recipient's access to college or vocational training. For example, in Washington and Benton Counties, nearly all scholarship recipients attend the University of Arkansas, Northwest Arkansas Community College, or the Northwest Technical Institute.

In almost every case, applicants have chosen career-directed majors or programs. These cover a wide spectrum of subject areas. For example, the 2000/2001 applicants in Washington County listed the following areas of study: nursing, surgical technology, teaching, journalism, computer programming, physics, accounting, graphic design, communications, social work, office technology, criminal justice, psychology, computer science, community health, business, Spanish, kinesiology, landscape architecture, zoology, organizational management, special education, human development, medical technology, interior design, political science, and pre-law. The fund does not provide scholarships for graduate school except for those earning a Master of Arts in Teaching (MAT) degree because the program is a five-year course of study.

While scholarship recipients experience a variety of changes as their studies progress, they consistently demonstrate an increasingly positive self-image. As they reapply each semester, they display what Ralph Nesson describes as "a more hopeful outlook on life" and a growing confidence in their abilities. Their resolve strengthens, as Deborah, a mother of two, expressed: "I knew I was going to complete school. Each semester I got stronger."

A mentoring program and a state-of-the-art, on-line financial-aid information service have been added to the scholarship program. Students are also given resource handbooks with important phone numbers for child care, food stamps, clothing, and shelter. In one county, low-interest loans were available for those needing car repairs. (As pointed out earlier, transportation is often a major problem for single parents.) Other students have received used computers through the program, donated by individuals and businesses. Several volunteers help to upgrade the computers so that they will serve the needs of students.

Essential in an age when they figure so heavily in education and the work world, the computers are provided for free to the scholarship recipients.

Today, the founders of the Single Parent Scholarship Fund of Washington County can look back with pride on a record of community involvement and caring whose successes have led to a statewide effort. The Scholarship Fund's clear purpose, a helpful board of directors, and strong vision were all necessary for the program to make the strides it has made and continues to make.

Getting Started

For the individual or group wanting to create a scholarship program, the first step in creating an organizational structure is to form a board of directors and develop a mission statement. In the case of the ASPSF, the board consists of eleven to twenty-one members who represent the entire state, both in geography and demographics. The makeup of the board is important, given the board's central role in translating the program's philosophy into action.

Board members should be able to assist with bringing in donations through both their professional and personal contacts. It is important to remember that board members can open doors that might otherwise be closed. Members of the business community can bring valuable expertise. Members who are well connected, who are adept at outreach and networking, and who are willing to speak on behalf of the program, are a must.

The size of the board should reflect the broad-based community support that is needed. A board that is too large or too small may be inefficient in utilizing the skills and expertise of its members. A strategic plan is essential in moving the vision forward, and without an active board movement of the plan cannot be accomplished.

Incorporation was also a key step in the Arkansas program's growth. Initially housed under several different tax-exempt organizations (e.g., the Office of Human Concern, EOA), the local county affiliates began to grow and decided to incorporate as a statewide organization, the Arkansas Single Parent Scholarship Fund, which began in 1992.[4] Incorporation serves to limit the legal and financial liability of individual staff and board members of each affiliate. This protection is important in the event of a lawsuit against the organization because the state organization and its assets become liable rather than individual leaders. Incorporation papers were filed with the Secretary of State's office, following legal advice provided free of charge.[5]

Next, every organization should have a written statement that clearly expresses its reasons for existence. A mission statement should focus upon the changes that the organization would like to see occur. The Arkansas Single Parent Scholarship Fund has a statement of purpose that reads:

> It is the mission of the Arkansas Single Parent Scholarship Fund to initiate and develop community-based incentive scholarship funds within the counties of Arkansas for the purpose of helping single parents enroll in institutions of higher learning, complete their studies, and achieve economic self-sufficiency through professional employment.

This statement appears in the constitution (the basic governing principles) and by-laws (the rules governing the details of internal affairs) of the Scholarship Fund. It is clear and reflects the changes that the organization would like to see occur. Further, it is concise and specific; too broad a mission statement might lead potential donors and volunteers to misread the goals of the organization.

The ASPSF drafted its constitution and by-laws early in its development, gaining approval by the board. These documents cover questions of purpose, criteria for board membership, board members' responsibilities and terms of office, organizational structure, meeting schedules, voting requirements, authority of officers, and procedures to be followed in amending the constitution and bylaws.[6]

The need of single parents for a strong support system is not taken lightly at the local and state level of the organization. Members of the board, including its director, are fully aware that it takes more than simply enrolling in college to be successful. Personal changes must also occur, and a safety net must be in place for single parents or the chances of success are limited. For this reason scholarship applicants are introduced to a myriad of resources—everything from where to go to get vouchers, food stamps, and housing assistance, to help in finding affordable child care, transportation, other scholarships, and mentors. In one county a grant was secured to provide case management and work with women individually to increase their feelings of empowerment and to build self-esteem. What this board seemed to understand is that formal education is only part of what poor single parents need.

Another important task is fund-raising. In discussions with board members and donors in Washington County, I learned that potential donors need to know what their money will support. While those who contribute regularly to nonprofits clearly possess a willingness to give, they still need to know why their talents and time are required. During interviews and focus groups with board members and donors, I began to sense a spirit of giving. This experience led me to reconsider my own understanding of community. I helped me to realize that ordinary citizens can make a difference starting at the most basic level.

Sociologists often view community as the junction where the individual and the broader society meet. We are all familiar with the phrase "a sense of community," which implies a feeling of belonging, solidarity, or connectedness to others. Similarly, most of us have heard of social critics who mourn the "loss of community," who sense that the social "glue" that once served to unite us has loosened. Having become involved with the scholarship program as a board member and gotten to know the individuals involved with the project, I can better understand the connection that I felt as a scholarship recipient. Moreover, my involvement has made me far more optimistic about what can be done at the grassroots level.

Sociologist Émile Durkheim argued that a sense of moral regulation and social obligation were essential to positive social interaction. In an ideal world, members of communities interact in accordance with their obligations to others and to society as a whole. I found this to be a strong theme among the diverse group of volunteers. Board members seemed to heed the call of Alexis de Tocqueville to be involved in civic duty. In his observation of American democracy, de Tocqueville concluded that the best bulwark against an isolationist and antagonistic society is civic association, community, and social ties. "A people amongst whom individuals should lose the power of achieving things single-handed, without acquiring the means of producing them by united exertions, would soon relapse into barbarism."[7] Those involved in the numerous affiliates around the state have worked together to create a collective civility that can be extended to those in need.

Hope, a retired professional who now calls herself a "professional volunteer," explained, "I work for about seventeen to twenty different organizations. As a volunteer you choose the programs that you believe in, that you feel are doing the most good." When I asked Hope about her involvement with the Single Parent Scholarship Fund, she credited her trust in the director. "But," she added, "from the start it's been run with every dollar counting." Deb, another board member, commented, "Everything is local, and I think that appeals to people [donors] because any donations here are local [intended for area recipients]. I think accountability is important too, and how you budget your money. People want to know that their money is being spent on the purpose for which it was intended. I know I do." Both Hope and Deb are board members and donors as well.

The value of education surfaced almost immediately as I spoke with board members. Gene, a retired professor, explained, "I was in higher education for forty-four years, and I believe in it, and I just think that if people educate themselves they'll have better lives and they'll contribute more to society. Any money that we invest in them will be just that, an investment. Just seeing them [scholarship recipients] progress is important." Another member added, "One thing my father always said was 'You can take away everything a person has, but you can't take away their education.' I admire the general stick-to-itiveness and motivation these single parents have."

The promotion of education is obviously consistent with another goal: helping to eliminate poverty. "I grew up in the Depression," Gene explains. "And some people are—I've got relatives that are embarrassed to talk about the fact that we were poor, but I'm not embarrassed at all. Everybody was poor. That helped, I suppose, but I think that once you've seen that, then you have a little more concern about what's happening to people out there."

Knowledge that the scholarship recipients are already in transition is another important element to giving. Board members explained on numerous occasions that knowing that single parents had initiated the process of change by applying for the scholarship and for admission to school had made it easier for them to contribute. "All we are doing is giving some assistance and support to people who are going to do 99 percent of the work themselves," one member explained. Another added, "It's always been the idea that you give folks help but with that help comes the expectation of change and progress, not just school, but internal change. We see the person's view of herself change and that's real important too."

Diane, a long-time board member, put it best when she said,

> One of the things that I find so rewarding . . . is that you
> know people come to us because they have decided they want
> a better life. Yes, some are more successful than others, but
> these are people that have made a decision, and often a very
> terrifying decision, to seek higher education. We hear them

over and over again tell us they didn't do well in high school, they dropped out, they got poor grades. And so it's a win/win situation for them, for their children, for society.

In Arkansas each affiliate has a unique approach to fundraising, which is no doubt the most difficult yet most crucial component of the program. After all, without money for scholarships, there is no fund. Indeed, the generation of scholarship funds is a never-ending endeavor, involving letters and personal visits to corporations, foundations, and individuals.

No doubt, the job of fundraising requires some level of sophistication, perhaps even charisma. I observed Ralph appeal to numerous groups for support, and I often stood in awe of his stamina and his skill as an advocate. Generating a continuing flow of support from both individuals and corporations requires persistent cultivation of potential donors and a willingness to accept "no" more times than one can imagine without becoming discouraged.

One fund-raising event that has been especially successful is the annual Holiday Gala. Every December in Washington County, donors and recipients are brought together for an evening of food, drink, and fellowship. The host is always a prominent member of the community. For several years this event has featured a challenge grant, which the director and board members work on throughout the year. The goal is to have a group of donors in place within the community who agree to match the amount raised during the gala. This event, which began with just a few thousand dollars in matching grants, has succeeded beyond the board's expectations. For example, the 1999 Christmas Gala for Washington County was held at the home of a local physician. The matching funds equaled $15,000.

Benefactors attend along with board members, and scholarship recipients are invited to the celebration as well. This may be the most effective aspect of the event. Donors listen to recipients speak in intervals throughout the evening. They tell something about their educational goals, their majors, the courses in which they are currently enrolled. It would be difficult to listen to them tell about their goals and dreams without feeling a sense of connection. Indeed, these are the moments when donors and potential donors are reminded why they participate in the Scholarship Fund. I remember speaking at such an event many years ago. I was nervous as I stood up and told the intimidating crowd, assembled in the home of a stranger, about my dreams and hopes for the future. I thanked them for their help and promised to do my best. Sociologists have written about the symbolic weight of "commitment rituals" and how they hold the potential to transform our lives. These are the moments that remain with us.

This year I watched a woman tell about her struggle with biology and how delighted she was to learn that she had gotten a B in the course. An older woman seated on a couch directly in front of the speaker had tears in her eyes. Later many came up to the scholarship recipient during the evening to express words of encouragement and to say that they were proud of her accomplishments. I listened to other single parents talk about how education was transforming their lives, how they had earned an A in marketing, physics, or sociology, and how they looked forward to the coming semester or graduation. Each talked about how much the scholarship meant to them personally. I listened as they assured a room of strangers that they were "on their way out of poverty" and thanked them for their generosity.

Other counties sponsor equally interesting fund-raisers. One is held in Newton County, an extremely poor, rural part of Arkansas that boasts some of the most beautiful scenery to be found in the Ozark Mountains. County affiliates created a tour of homes that is held each year during the holiday season. Often the homes are very secluded, nestled deep in the mountains. Tickets to the tour are sold by the board members, and participants drive at their leisure from home to home, sip hot chocolate or cider, and all the while enjoy the breathtaking views.

Other affiliates have held spaghetti suppers, an "all-you-can-eat shrimp and crab fest," golf tournaments, raffles, auctions, bake sales, dances, and fashion shows. In one county, sixth graders at a local middle school raised funds for various community projects and included the Single Parent Scholarship Fund among their recipients. Likewise, local newspapers, television, and radio can be important allies. In each of these events, strategic planning and hard work on the part of board members were key.

Corporate Giving

Once the scholarship fund is fully established, corporate giving becomes a real possibility. State and federal grants and corporations will likely be the bulk of the income as a fund grows. It is important to remember that corporations have a very public need to give. The larger the corporation, the greater its need to create a positive public image. Surveys have found that a growing segment of the population agrees with the statement, "As they grow bigger, companies usually get cold and impersonal in their relationship with people." Indeed, the proportion agreeing with this statement increased from 55 percent in the late 1950s to almost 80 percent by 1985.[8]

Philanthropy is a way to demonstrate a corporation's good will and its commitment to social responsibility. Smaller businesses and corporations do not suffer the image problems of larger corporations, in part because they are perceived as being closer to the community. Larger corporations have a strong need to convince the public that while they earn substantial profits, they often redistribute a significant portion of those profits to the community for selfless goals.

It is a worthwhile effort to assist corporations in realizing that the success of graduates is not only evidence of corporate money well spent; it also increases the pool of educated potential employees. For example, in Washington County, the Scholarship Fund has been assisted by Tyson Foods, Wal-Mart, and numerous other corporations for whom many former scholarship recipients now work. Donors of all types like to be appreciated, and public acknowledgment of corporate contributions is also welcome publicity for the donor. Including corporate management in board make-up can also boost the adage, "The closer you are to the corporation, the closer you are to the gift." Remember this when constructing a board. Board members can contribute to your success in various ways, from always being available to make phone calls, to serving as mentors, to making donations, to contacting others in their community. Members may not be able to contribute a significant sums of money, but their expertise and network of contacts may be of great value.

Other potential large donors include local philanthropists and community foundations. Generosity at this level requires special thanks and recognition. In addition, local philanthropists can have great influence upon other members of the community. Their approval of your project may well lead others to want to support you. For example, in both Benton and Washington Counties, matching grants from the Community Care Foundation, the Walton Family Foundation, and the Bernice and Harvey Jones Foundation have been strongly supported by others in the community who respect their choices.

It is equally important to respect anonymous donors, especially those making large contributions. Indeed, one of the points made during a focus group with board members and donors of the Scholarship Fund was that giving is a very personal decision for many, and it can be a touchy subject if boundaries of privacy are crossed.

The potential scholarship fund organizer must remember that individuals and corporations give to successful programs. Starting a Single Parent Scholarship Fund will require a long-term commitment to develop public visibility and a positive reputation, but it is worth the effort.[9] The Arkansas Single Parent Scholarship has a proven record after sixteen years. Starting a new organization will require patience and understanding combined with the belief that communities really can make a difference in the lives of single parent families. Until policy makers, politicians, and service providers acknowledge the increasing demands on single parents, and the necessity of education to lift these families out of poverty, they will remain an invisible group.[10] Single parent scholarship funds in communities across the nation have the potential to build strong scaffolds upon which single parents can stand, helping them to reach heights they might otherwise never imagine.

7 Where Do We Go from Here?

Throughout this book I have attempted to show by example how education can change the lives of single mothers and their children and why obtaining a post-secondary degree is so important. In retrospect, the worlds of poverty from which they came can be seen as a temporary obstacle. Today, these women are empowered, filled with new hope, and better equipped to cope with the challenges they will continue to face.

It is worth remembering that these women were already working hard before they decided to continue their educations. Many people assume that poor children are housed in families where parents could work but choose not to. Yet, in reality, most poor families do work for wages. Even among those receiving welfare assistance, nearly 50 percent include a parent who worked for wages during the preceding year. For example, during the mid-1990s, about 56,000 families with children were classified as poor in Arkansas, despite the fact that 76.7 percent had one or more working adults. Of that number, 27.3 percent worked full-time year-round.[1] This is just above the national average of 25.2 percent of poor families in the same category. In other words, of more than 6 million poor families with children in the United States, over 1.5 million of those families had at least one full-time, year-round worker.[2] Many of those were receiving some form of welfare.

In Arkansas over half a million parents were working, but more than one-third (36 percent) earned hourly wages too low to lift a family of four out of poverty.[3] Though states can further increase the minimum wage, several have not done so. Arkansas does not stand alone in this. Families in other states, including Alabama, Arizona, Idaho, Kentucky, Louisiana, Mississippi, the Dakotas, Texas, West Virginia, and Wyoming experience similarly high percentages of working poor.

Despite the prospect of low-wage labor that awaits those transitioning from welfare to work, recent federal policy has emphasized reduction of the welfare rolls, moving families into the workplace and off government assistance. The success of this policy will depend greatly upon the skills and education welfare recipients take with them into the workplace. Otherwise they will move from welfare poor to working poor, a group that federal policy has yet to address. Early research examining the earnings of former welfare recipients has begun to reveal a bleak picture of those who leave welfare to join the ranks of the working poor.[4] In their study of welfare mothers, Edin and Lein (1997) found that even though most poor mothers reported being happier working, they were not better off financially. Despite their determination to work and not use welfare, most were forced back onto the rolls for a time because of the punitive nature of low-wage work.[5] Typical welfare-to-work programs are moving people off welfare, but only into jobs that provide a few hundred dollars' increase in income.[6] The danger of TANF is that when low-wage jobs are lost, single parents cannot return for temporary assistance, as they could with AFDC. Any illusion of a safety net is now gone.[7]

Edin and Lein (1997) found that while working mothers earned more income than they had received on welfare, they also reported much higher expenditures and, thus, greater hardships. This is extremely problematic given that unskilled single mothers with children are at the highest risk of poverty, more than any other group in the United States. In this chapter, I examine current policy suggestions aimed at both reducing poverty and increasing access to higher education.

Policy and Poverty

Public discussion of such policy proposals as raising the minimum wage, creating affordable, high-quality child care, establishing state-level earned-income tax credits, expanding access to health insurance, and strengthening unemployment insurance has moved off center stage. Poor families have once again become invisible as middle-class tax cuts and a "hands-off" approach toward governing now rule the public arena.

From 1993 to 1995, disposable incomes rose substantially for families headed by single mothers. Yet despite continued economic growth and expansion of the federal earned-income tax credit (EITC), after 1995 the incomes of the poorest fifth of single mother families fell as they were dropped from TANF and lost their eligibility for food stamps.[8] Analysts argue that the drop in means-tested program participation far exceeded the decline in need. This may have happened, in part, through poor case management; clients may have been forced into work settings that were not a good fit for their capabilities. Such practices may ultimately result in clients returning to the starting line but without a safety net because of reduced time limits. Indeed, between 1995 and 1997, the number of TANF recipients fell by 3 million (22.2 percent) nationwide. Yet, the number of individuals in single mother families classified as poor prior to receiving public assistance fell by only 5.4 percent. During this same period, the number of people receiving food stamps fell by 16.6 percent while those in poverty fell by only 2.9 percent.[9]

The Center on Budget and Policy Priorities has identified five policy options that states could implement to assist poor families. These include creating a state earned-income tax credit; raising the state minimum wage; modifying cash-assistance rules so that benefits are phased out gradually as a family's earnings rise; strengthening unemployment insurance to improve eligibility for low-wage workers; and improving access to services such as child care and health insurance.

A state earned-income tax credit (EITC) has been adopted in more than a dozen states but has yet to become universal.[10] The state tax credit is designed to supplement the federal earned-income tax credit, which is intended to help offset payroll taxes and reduce the costs to moderate- and low-income workers. The refundable credit (a specified percentage of the EITC) would supplement wages for low-income workers. For example, it would work similarly to the federal EITC, providing refund checks to families where the EITC exceeds a family's tax bill. Making tax-preparation services available could help many poor families receive their tax credits in a timely fashion.

According to the Center on Budget and Policy Priorities, low-income families pay a substantially larger proportion of their wages to local and state governments than middle- and upper-income families because of regressive sales and excise taxes. Thus, the state earned-income tax credit can help those families who remain poor even after receiving the federal tax credit and "complement efforts to help families make the transition from welfare to work."[11]

It is important to reconsider the official poverty threshold currently in place as well as the minimum wage. A more accurate measure of how much income is required to cover basic needs should be established and implemented nationwide. In 1999 the organization Arkansas Advocates for Children and Families established what it calls the Family Income Standard (FIS). This measure is used to determine the income an Arkansas family requires in order to meet its basic needs without government and charitable assistance. Not surprisingly, the figure (about 185 percent above the official poverty level) is much higher than what a worker paid the current federal minimum wage of $5.15 per hour can earn. Today, one adult earning the minimum wage is automatically below the poverty level if he or she has at least one child.

Popular images of minimum-wage workers feature teenagers working at Burger King and McDonald's. In truth, however, most minimum wage workers are adults. And although the 1998 increase in federal minimum wage to $5.15 per hour is a step in the right direction, the value of the increase, once adjusted for inflation, is lower than any time in the past 30 years. For the minimum wage to reach the purchasing power it had in the 1970s, it would have to be well above $7.00 per hour.[12] One study found that in Arkansas, a single parent family with one child would need an hourly wage of at least $8.90 per hour to cover its basic needs. The amount would be higher in states with a higher cost of living.[13]

While a few states have taken action to raise their minimum wage above the federal level, in most there is a fear that raising wage levels will result in a net loss in jobs. The worry is that supply of labor costs will cause employers to demand less of it. Evidence doesn't support this but the rhetoric is strong.[14] Obviously, those who would most benefit from higher minimum wages are the millions of low-wage workers and those being transitioned from welfare to work. In lieu of raising wages, some states have attempted to slow the phasing of reduced welfare benefits so as to provide income boosts to welfare recipients who are finding work (for example, through extended child care or medical coverage). These are called "enhanced earnings disregards" whereby clients can earn a certain amount above the poverty line without losing benefits completely.

Because periods of unemployment have such negative effects on the poor, the Center on Budget and Policy Priorities has recommended that unemployment insurance be strengthened. In the past decade federal and state governments have made unemployment insurance more restrictive. A smaller number of workers receive unemployment insurance today for a variety of reasons, such as limited eligibility, a decline in manufacturing, and increase in service jobs (more likely to be part-time or intermittent). For example, in Arkansas, only about 27,000 of the eligible 59,000 workers, or 45 percent, received unemployment benefits in 1995.[15]

One limitation of unemployment insurance is that workers who voluntarily leave a job are ineligible for benefits regardless of the reason. This rule has implications for single parents who are unable to work when their child care or transportation arrangements break down, a common occurrence for poor single parents. Indeed, research has shown that many welfare recipients were formerly working but quit or lost jobs due to problems with child care.[16] In these cases, unemployment benefits were denied even though their decision to leave work was hardly voluntary. More regard for such legitimate and unavoidable setbacks is needed when determining eligibility for services.

Asset accumulation is especially problematic for low-income families. While there are state and federal policies designed to encourage asset accumulation (for example, mortgage supports or incentives for retirement savings), those who benefit are largely middle- and upper-income families. Meanwhile, low-income families are often penalized when they try to save or build assets. For example, those receiving food stamps, Medicaid, or TANF (TEA in Arkansas) are unable to have savings, retirement or pension accounts, bonds, or stocks. TANF allows a family only $3,000 in resources, an amount that is often too low to weather emergencies.[17]

Our net worth (assets minus debts) is more accurate an indicator of true wealth than our incomes. And as Table 7.1 reveals, while the gap between the richest and poorest families has narrowed slightly, in 1998 the average net worth of the richest families in the United States remained 142 times that of the poorest families.

An especially empowering project that has taken off in more than a dozen communities (including in Arkansas) is

Table 7.1   U.S. Families' Net Worth by Income Level, 1989 and 1998 (dollars)

Income	1989	1998
< 10,000	1,900	3,600
10,000–24,999	22,800	24,800
25,000–49,999	58,100	60,300
50,000–99,999	131,400	152,000
100,000 and higher	542,100	510,800

Source: "Recent Changes in U.S. Family Finances: Results from the 1998 Survey of Consumer Finances." *Federal Reserve Bulletin,* January 2000. Cited in "Self-sufficiency: Assets as Critical as Income." Arkansas Working Families Project, July 2000, No. 2.

the Individual Development Account (IDA). The Corporation for Enterprise Development has put into action a $15 million demonstration project called "Downpayment on the American Dream," whereby poor families can accrue assets through tax-exempt accounts.[18] The savings may be used for education, home purchases, retirement pensions, or for starting a business. Government or private agencies agree to match the contributions made by individuals, sometimes as much as threefold.[19]

Access to Post-Secondary Education

Prior to the 1970s, many Americans believed that education could loosen the connection between an individual's class and their class origins by enhancing their success in the labor market. In other words, we believed that education would resolve the problem of inequality if it were made available to everyone. In keeping with the spirit of the times, college admissions policies began to emphasize diversity as a way to address the problem of unequal access to higher education. By the late 1970s, however, the move to democratize education had begun to be challenged. In the mid-1980s the National Commission of Excellence in Education reported that the United States was at risk because of a rising tide of "mediocrity" in education. The debate polarized the virtues of excellence and equality, and the resulting backlash continues today.

Affirmative action, intended to further the democratization process, has always drawn criticism but never so much as it did in the 1990s. Colleges are now being forced to reverse decisions to admit students based upon minority status, claiming that such preferential policies constitute "reverse discrimination." Moreover, critics claim that institutionalized discrimination and prejudice are a thing of the past, and that the playing field is now level. Not surprisingly, college attendance by minorities has declined sharply at those universities that have ended affirmative action.[20]

Defenders of affirmative action have argued that the African American middle class, especially, has benefited from such programs, in spite of the fact that educational opportunity has yet to produce economic opportunity for all racial minorities. But while education assists all groups, race continues to be a factor in earnings differential. In other words, holding education constant, women and minorities still earn less than their white male counterparts. Proponents of affirmative action in education and hiring argue that racism remains deeply embedded in the fabric of society. Simply endorsing the principle of colorblindness does not assure that everyone will be able to compete fairly.

Still others argue that those who have benefited from campus affirmative-action policies are members of groups who are already most advantaged. For this reason some favor affirmative-action policies based on class rather than race or ethnicity, arguing that a class-based affirmative action policy would promote both class and racial equality.

Regardless of where one stands on the issue of affirmative action and open admissions, research has shown that educational attainment remains the single most important influence on job success. For this reason admission policies are significant in determining who will go on to experience occupational rewards. "B.A. holders appear far better off in status and earnings than those with high school diplomas."[21] The advantages are less clear for those with some college or associates' degrees.

Unfortunately, as I mentioned in Chapter 4, race and gender inequalities are not eradicated by educational achievement. Most startling, for example, is the fact that among women and minorities, only white women with advanced and professional degrees earn more than white males with high school diplomas. And while the differences narrow with educational levels, differences in earnings between minority workers and their white male counterparts remain significant.

Policies will have to change to make education as broadly accessible in reality as it is in our minds. During the 1990s, cuts in financial aid and shifts in the types of available aid, away from grants and toward the increased use of loans, have had adverse effects upon low-income students. Many needy students attending college must also work full- or part-time in order to remain in school. Research has shown that working reduces the likelihood of graduation or delays it by two to three years. This has important implications for single parents, who typically need to enter the workforce as soon as possible. For them, delaying graduation likely means prolonging poverty. In addition, the longer it takes to complete a bachelor's degree, the less likely one is to earn an advanced degree.[22]

There are several options that financial aid agencies and campuses could pursue to help reduce the costs of higher education for single parents. One example might be to rethink the distribution of financial aid. Pell grants and supplemental grants could offer larger allowances for students with one or more dependents, which would enable single parent students to borrow less to complete their educations. The income-tax deduction for college tuition is helpful but does not go far enough. Admissions and financial-aid offices could have counselors on hand to help with the acquisition of transcripts, completion of other admission procedures, and the aid application process, procedures which many returning students find overwhelming.

A cooperative on-site child care facility could offer sliding-scale fees for those unable to afford private child care. These facilities could utilize the skills of single parents, who could work at the facility a certain number of hours each week in return for free child care.

Expanded course offerings are much needed on university campuses, which still schedule classes with traditional students in mind. While many community colleges have begun to offer evening and weekend courses, most universities have yet to provide this needed service. Often single parents can only arrange affordable child care in the evenings, with the help of extended family members who work during the day. Weekend and evening course offerings could help ease the child-care burden for many families.

Remedial courses are often needed for students who are ill prepared for college. While these programs are controversial, they are necessary if universities and community colleges are truly committed to the goal of education for all. Critics argue that offerings in remedial math, reading, and science, as well as study skills and time management, constitute a "dumbing down" of the curriculum. I strongly disagree with this assessment. First, graduation credit is not offered for these courses. Students who opt to enroll in them still have to take the full range of courses required for their major. Second, students come to college with very diverse cultural baggage. Many single parents either have not completed high school and arrive with just a GED in hand, or they have been out of school long enough that they require some retooling. Indeed, I would argue that there is even justification for offering courses on self-esteem building, résumé construction, and assertiveness training. Single parents also often arrive in college with handicaps related to low self-esteem. Unfortunately, the universities that do offer these transitional programs do not always receive recognition for their efforts. Some faculty and administrators tend to raise an eyebrow when they encounter students who have taken these courses, adding stigma to an already difficult transition into college life.

Research has shown that one factor that accounts for differences between males and females in their choice of an academic major is their assessment of the job market and their perception of what they can realistically aspire to. Career counseling and mentoring programs can help expand horizons for women entering the university setting. Moving into occupations that are traditionally held by males will mean increased earning potential overall.

Currently, the state of Washington is considering legislation that would give low-income working parents training credits that could be used for higher education. The "earned income training credits," as they are called, could be applied directly toward college tuition, or used to reimburse employers who provide education and training. Other organizations are involved in this move toward "life-long learning."[23]

Campus housing for single parent families could help create a supportive community, which might provide not only valuable social networks to single parents but perhaps such tangible services as on-site child care. While many universities do provide married student housing, the needs of single parent families are unique.

Finally, and perhaps most important, as I mentioned in Chapter 3, the work requirements mandated in the 1996 welfare-reform law preclude most welfare recipients from getting a post-secondary education. Moreover, the law restricts what states are able to do on their own by requiring that a certain proportion of recipients be employed or engaged in "work-related activities." (This proportion is set to be 50 percent by 2002.) In most cases, states cannot consider more than one year of job-related education or training as "work," although a few states have taken the initiative to expand this to two years. This policy will have to change to make a real difference in the lives of single parents and their children.

Combined, these suggested programs and policy changes could help to reduce some of the challenges that single parents face today. With stronger support, single parents who have yet to consider pursuing higher education may find this a plausible option. The only statewide program of its kind, the Arkansas Single Parent Scholarship Fund, is an excellent first step in making post-secondary education possible for single parents journeying up and out of poverty.

Appendix A

*Constitution and Bylaws
of the Arkansas Single Parent
Scholarship Fund*

Article One: Introduction

The name of this Corporation shall be the Arkansas Single Parent Scholarship Fund, Inc.

Impoverished single parents in Arkansas as elsewhere face a bleak and discouraging future without adequate education and job skills. Left with the major responsibility for rearing their children, they cannot compete in the job market for well-paying jobs if they have not gone beyond high school. The result for many is low self-esteem, welfare dependence, semi-skilled employment, substandard housing, and other extreme difficulties stemming from involuntary poverty. For some, unwanted teen pregnancy is the first step on the path toward single parent impoverishment. The pattern repeats itself all too often in subsequent generations. In other cases, separation, divorce, or a spouse's death reduces the family's income to a subsistence level. Regardless of the cause, the net result is economic disadvantage with all its harmful effects. The Arkansas Single Parent Scholarship Fund is an effort to support low-income single parents who aspire to a better life through education.

Article Two: Purpose

This Corporation is and shall be operated as a nonprofit corporation pursuant to Arkansas Acts of 1963, No. 175 and it shall have the following objects and purposes:

119

1. To initiate and develop community-based incentive scholarship funds within the state of Arkansas for the purpose of helping impoverished single parents enroll in institutions of higher learning, complete their studies, and achieve economic self-sufficiency through professional employment.

2. To develop support systems for scholarship recipients in order that maximum community assistance be available to single parent students.

3. To generate financial resources for scholarship funds through appeals for corporate, foundation, and individual contributions within Arkansas and throughout the United States.

4. To engage in charitable, civic, social, and educational work of any nature permitted by law deemed beneficial to scholarship recipients, communities served, and to society as a whole.

Article Three: Board Structure and Organization

1. Annual fiscal and program year: The annual fiscal and program year of the Arkansas Single Parent Scholarship Fund shall commence January 1st and end December 31st.

2. Membership: The membership shall be no fewer than 11 members and no more than 21 members. The board will be considered full with 11 or more members. A quorum shall be 50 percent of the board membership at any particular time. (AS AMENDED)

3. Board selection: In recognition of the statewide emphasis of the Fund, positions on the board of directors shall be representative of all areas of Arkansas and shall reflect its racial, ethnic, and economic diversity. The board president shall appoint a nominating committee for the purpose of filling vacancies. New members shall be elected in September and seated in January. If at any time during the year, the total board membership should fall below twenty-one, the board may nominate, elect, and seat new members before the regular annual process. A majority vote of the board is required to seat any new member. (AS AMENDED)

4. Terms and Rotation:

A. Founding board members shall draw positions in January, 1992 for transitional terms, with:

- seven members serving until December, 1992
- seven members serving until December, 1993
- seven members serving until December, 1994

B. Initial terms of the restructured board shall be established as follows:
  - seven members shall begin terms in January, 1993 to serve until January, 1995
  - seven members shall begin terms in January, 1994 to serve until December, 1996
  - seven members shall begin terms in January, 1995 to serve until December, 1997

C. Regular rotation of three-year terms will begin in January, 1993 with one-third of the membership to be selected annually. No member may serve more than two consecutive three-year terms. (AS AMENDED)

5. Vacancies: If by resignation of members the total board membership should fall below 21 at any time, the president shall appoint a special nominating committee (which may consist of the executive committee) to propose new member(s) for consideration by the full board. The new board member shall serve the remainder of the term of the member who has been replaced and shall be eligible for election for one subsequent term on the board.

6. Resignation or Removal : A board member may resign at any time by delivering a written resignation to the president or to the (administrative) director of the corporation. A board member may be removed from service on the board of directors for the following reasons:

A. Chronic absence at board meetings, defined as missing three meetings in any calendar year or missing three meetings in a row without just cause;

B. Lack of interest in continuing to serve;

C. Conflict of interest or misconduct: no board member of this Corporation shall use her/his position as such to secure privileges or exemptions for her/himself or others, or have any interest, financial or otherwise, directly or beneficially, or engage in any business transaction or professional activity or incur any obligation of any nature which is in substantial conflict with the proper discharge of her/his duties in the Corporation's interest. Board members may be removed from their position with the Corporation when found to be in violation of the above provision.

7. Committees: The board of directors, by resolution adopted by a majority of the directors, may designate and appoint an executive committee which shall consist of the board president and at least two other board members. The executive committee shall have and exercise the authority to act on the board's behalf, and in lieu of action by the full board of directors when necessary and expedient, provided that actions taken by the executive committee be deemed final only upon ratification by the full board of directors at a subsequent meeting where a quorum is present.

Other committees not having and exercising the authority of the board of directors may be appointed by the president. All committees appointed by the president shall be composed of at least two directors. Additional persons other than directors may be appointed to committees. All committee members shall be appointed by, and serve at the pleasure of, the president of the board of directors.

8. Officers: The board of directors shall organize itself by the election of a president, vice-president, a secretary and treasurer and such other officers as it may deem useful. Election of such officers shall be for terms of one year, beginning January 1 and ending December 31st. Each officer shall serve until a successor is elected or appointed and qualified, or until her/his resignation or removal from office. Officers elected by the board of directors shall not serve more than two years in succession in a specific office. Officers elected or appointed by the board may resign at any time by delivering a letter to the president or the (administrative) director. (AS AMENDED)

Officers may be removed for cause at any time by the board through a two-thirds majority vote of the directors present at any regular or special meeting properly called with a quorum present. The removed officer will remain a member of the board of directors unless additional action as provided for in Article 3(5) is taken.

Except as may otherwise be provided in these bylaws, a vacancy occurring in any office provided for in this section shall be filled by the board of directors for the unexpired portion of the term of service, and no office shall be left vacant more than ninety (90) days.

The president shall preside at all meetings of the board of directors. The president may sign any deeds, mortgages, bonds, contracts, or other instruments which the board of directors has authorized to be executed, except in cases where the signing and execution thereof shall be delegated by the board of directors to the (administrative) director; and in general shall perform all duties incident to the office of president and such other duties as may be prescribed by the board of directors from time to time.

In the absence of the president or in the event of an inability or refusal to act, the vice-president shall perform the duties of the president, and when so acting, shall have all the powers of and be subject to all the restrictions upon the president. The vice-president shall perform such other duties as from time to time may be assigned by the president or by the board of directors.

The secretary shall record and transcribe the minutes prior to their being mailed to board members; see that all notices are duly given in accordance with provisions of these bylaws or as required by law; and perform such other duties as may from time to time be assigned by the president or the board of directors.

The treasurer shall review and present corporate financial statements and the annual independent financial audit to the board of directors; and perform such other duties as may from time to time be assigned by the president or the board of directors.

9. Meetings: Regular meetings of the board of directors shall be three times per year in January, April, and July at times and places determined by the board president to be convenient for all board members to attend. A fourth meeting for planning and review purposes shall be scheduled during the month of October. Board members shall be notified of any and all regular board meetings by first class letter mailed to each individual director; posting of such letter with correct postage and placing in the proper receptacle of the U.S. Postal Service shall be deemed sufficient notification, when such posting is accomplished at least ten (10) days but not more than twenty-one (21) days in advance. (AS AMENDED)

Special meetings of the board of directors may be called by the board president or by a simple majority vote of the executive committee when immediate action of the full board is deemed necessary. Written notification of special meetings shall include the purpose of the meeting and be accomplished at least five (5) days in advance of the meeting.

Meetings of the executive committee may be held at any such time as the board president shall officially call, using the first class mail notification procedure stated above and accomplished at least five (5) days in advance of the scheduled meeting. Emergency meetings of the executive committee may be held by telephone conference call and shall not be subject to written advance notification requirements.

10. Special provisions: The board of directors shall cause to be observed and are themselves subject to the following special provisions:

- A. At any official meeting of the board, a quorum of fifty percent (50%) of the current membership (with vacancies deducted from the total) of the board is required for the transaction of business; the act of a simple majority of the directors present at such a meeting shall be the act of the board of directors, as may be otherwise provided by law, the Articles of Incorporation, or these bylaws. (AS AMENDED)
- B. Any action required by law to be taken at a meeting of the directors, or any action which could be taken at an official meeting of the directors, may be taken without a meeting if a consent in writing setting forth the action so taken, shall be signed by all of the directors.
- C. There shall be no proxy voting by the board of directors.
- D. Members of the board of directors shall not receive any salary or wages for their services but may be reimbursed for any out-of-pocket reasonable expense incurred on behalf of the Corporation, including the costs of attending official board meetings. Nothing in these bylaws shall preclude the payment of board service honorarium in such amounts as the board may choose to establish.
- E. No member of any director's immediate family shall be employed by the Corporation. For purposes of these bylaws, the "immediate family" shall include such director's spouse, father, mother, brother, sister, son, daughter, father-in-law, mother-in-law, brother-in-law, sister-in-law, son-in-law, or daughter-in-law.
- F. The board of directors shall require those who are authorized to receive or expend funds be Bonded.

Article Four: Board Responsibilities

Section 1: General Authority

A. The powers of this Corporation shall be vested in a board of directors which shall determine major personnel, fiscal, and program policies, shall approve overall program plans and priorities and shall assure compliance with conditions of and approve proposals for financial assistance under the regulations governing the administration of grants, moneys, or gifts from any source.

B. The board of directors is responsible for and has authority over enforcement of all lawful provisions of the Corporation's charter.

C. The board, or its delegated agent, shall serve, for all required purposes, as the contracting party with the United States and agencies thereof, with states and political subdivisions thereof, or with other nonprofit corporations and private entities as appropriate; and as the contracting party, shall seek all necessary resources for the development, conduct, and administration of all programs determined to be in keeping with the goals of the Corporation and in the public interest.

D. The board of directors shall apply all provisions of Equal Opportunity Act regulations and, within these provisions, shall appoint an (administrative) director who shall be empowered to assemble, employ, disemploy, reorganize, and otherwise solely supervise those staff components that the board shall determine are necessary to forward the objectives of the Corporation.

E. The board of directors is hereby empowered to take any and all actions necessary for the continuance of the Corporation for that period of time set out in the Charter.

F. The board shall cause to be kept such official records as it may deem necessary but not less than the following:

(1) A minute book containing the official minutes of each regular or special meeting of the board of directors, and the official membership of the board of directors, brought current to the date of the regular board meeting.

(2) Annual budget and a complete accounting system which, among other things, shall be in compliance with all laws, rules, and regulations of any agency or regulatory body having jurisdiction over the business of the Corporation.

(3) An annual audit of the accounts and records of the Corporation by an independent qualified auditor, to be accomplished within 120 days after the end of the corporate year, or as required by a grantor for a specific program with required copies of such audit when approved by the board, forwarded by the auditor to the proper grantor(s).

(4) A personnel manual setting out regulations pertaining to all employees of the Corporation, notwithstanding that the (administrative) director shall serve at the pleasure of the board.

G. The board shall require those in the Corporation who are authorized to receive or expend funds to be Bonded.

Section 2

The duties and powers of the board of directors as outlined above shall not be subject to concurrence, veto, or modification by any other officials or authority except as stated herein, when altogether in compliance with the statutes regulating non-profit corporations in Arkansas.

Article Five: Indemnification

Section 1: Director/Officer Indemnification

The Corporation shall indemnify every person who is or has been a director or officer of the Corporation and such persons' heirs and legal representatives where such person is a party or is threatened with being made a party to any threatened, pending or completed action, suit or proceedings, whether civil, criminal, administrative or investigative, including all appeals, by reason of the fact that such person is or was director or officer of the Corporation, or is or was serving at the request of the Corporation in any capacity for any other business organization, against expenses (including attorneys' fees), judgment, decrees, fines, penalties, and amounts paid in settlement actually and reasonably incurred by such person in good faith and in a manner he reasonably believed to be in or not opposed to the best interests of the Corporation, and, with respect to any criminal action or proceeding, had no reasonable cause to believe his conduct was unlawful. The termination of any action, suit or proceeding by judgment, order, settlement, conviction or upon plea of nolo contendere or its equivalent, shall not of itself create a presumption that the person did not act in good faith or in a manner which he reasonably believed to be in or not opposed to the best interests of the Corporation or, with respect to any criminal action, suit or proceeding, that he had reasonable cause to believe that his conduct was unlawful. The foregoing right of indemnification shall be in addition to all rights to which any such director or officer may be entitled as a matter of law.

Section 2: Insurance

The Corporation may purchase and maintain insurance on its own behalf or on behalf of any person who is or was a director or officer of the Corporation or is or was serving at the request of the Corporation in any capacity for any other business organization, insuring the Corporation and such person against any liability asserted against such person and incurred by him in any such capacity, or arising out of his status as such, whether or not the Corporation would have the power to indemnify such person against such liability under the provisions of this bylaw or applicable law.

Article Six: The Director

The director shall exercise full authority for the administration and direction of the corporation within the policy developed by the board of directors. The director's authority and responsibility shall include, but not be limited to, the areas of:

A. Administration and Direction
(1) Assisting new and existing community-based single parent scholarship funds to develop throughout the state of Arkansas.
(2) Providing staff service to the board of directors, including preparation of agendas in consultation with the president.
(3) Preparing budgets for the operation of the Corporation.
(4) Locating funding sources and preparing proposals and applications for same.

(5) Developing relationships with other bodies for future funding and general liaison functions.

(6) Planning and preparing with appropriate board committees and staff the following: Reports on current activities, plans and problems for the board of directors.

(7) Coordinating corporation activities with all appropriate governmental and private agencies.

(8) Disbursement of all funds necessary for proper administration of all the Corporations' programs.

(9) Within the limits of established board policy, sign documents on behalf of the Corporation.

(10) Coordinate and organize special projects as directed by the board.

B. Staff:

(1) Supervision of all staff.

(2) Hiring and dismissal of staff subject to such conditions and policies as the board of directors may from time to time determine.

(3) Initiate such problem solving action as may be necessary to situations not covered by written personnel policy.

(4) Develop and administer training programs for staff as appropriate.

Article Seven: Amendments

These bylaws may be altered, amended, or repealed or rewritten by action adopted by a two-thirds majority of the directors present at any regular meeting at which a quorum is present, provided that the proposed amendments or action has been circulated to all board members at the time of the call for the meeting.

Amendments to the Constitution and Bylaws of the Arkansas Single Parent Scholarship Fund

First Amendment

1. The Corporation will distribute its income for each tax year at such time and in such manner as to not become subject to the tax on undistributed income imposed by Section 4942 of the Internal Revenue Code, or corresponding section of any future federal tax code.

2. The Corporation will not engage in any act of self-dealing as defined in Section 4941 of the Internal Revenue Code, or corresponding section of any future federal tax code.

3. The Corporation will not retain any excess building holding as defined in Section 4943(c) of the Internal Revenue code, or corresponding section of any future federal tax code.

4. The Corporation will not make any investments in such a manner as to subject it to tax under Section 4944 of the Internal Revenue Code, or corresponding section of any future federal tax code.

5. The Corporation will not make any taxable expenditures as defined in Section 4945(d) of the Internal Revenue Code, or corresponding section of any future federal tax code.

Second Amendment

Matching grants to participating county-level Single Parent Scholarship Funds will be extended upon receipt of signed statements to the effect that applicant selection committee members will abstain from the selection process if any relative is an applicant. The definition of relatives includes parent, grandparent, step-parent, sibling, cousin, mother- or father-in-law, sister- or brother-in-law, nephew, niece, child, or grandchild.

Third Amendment

Article 3, Section 8, Paragraph 1—Officers: The board of directors shall organize itself by election of a president, vice-president, secretary, and treasurer and such other officers as it may deem necessary.

Article 3, Section 9, Paragraph 1—Meetings: Regular meetings of the board of directors shall be three times per year in January, April, and July at times and places determined by the board president to be convenient for all board members to attend. A fourth meeting for planning and review purposes shall be scheduled during the month of October.

Article 3, Section 9, Paragraph 6: The secretary shall transcribe the minutes prior to their being mailed to board members, see that all notices are duly given in accordance with provisions of these bylaws or as required by law, and perform such other duties as may from time to time be assigned by the president of the board of directors.

The treasurer shall review and present corporate financial statements and the annual independent financial audit to the board of directors and perform such other duties as may from time to time be assigned by the president or the board of directors.

Appendix B

Nonprofit Resources

Web Sites

The Internet Nonprofit Center: www.nonprofits.org

Nonprofit Gateway: www.nonprofit.gov

Nonprofit Times: www.nptimes.com

Nonprofit Genie Homepage: www.genie.org

National Center for Nonprofit Boards: www.ncnb.org

Nonprofit Online News: www.gilbert.org

National Council on Nonprofit Associations: www.ncna.org

The Nonprofit Resource Center: www.not-for-profit.org

The Nonprofit Yellow Pages: www.npyp.net

Philanthropy Search: www.philanthropysearch.com

The Nonprofit ToolKit: www.nptoolkit.org

Nonprofit Tech: www.nonprofit-tech.org

Note: All web sites were verified to be accurate as of October 2001.

Publications

Bauer, David, G. 1995. *The "How To" Grants Manual.* Phoenix, Ariz.: Oryx Press.

Baumgartner, J. E. 1995. *National Directory of Grantmaking Public Charities.* New York: Foundation Center.

Bernstein, Susan R. 1991. *Managing Contracted Services in the Nonprofit Agency: Administrative, Ethical and Political Issues.* Philadelphia: Temple University Press.

131

Burlingame, Dwight, and Lamont Hulse. 1991. *Taking Fund Raising Seriously: Advancing the Profession and Practice of Raising Money.* San Francisco: Jossey-Bass.

Carver, John. 1990. *Boards That Make a Difference: A New Design for Leadership in Nonprofit and Public Organizations.* San Francisco: Jossey-Bass.

Chatterjee, Pranab, and Albert J. Abromovitz. 1993. *Structure of Nonprofit Management: A Casebook.* New York: Lanham.

Cohen, Lilly, and Dennis R. Young. 1989. *Careers for Dreamers and Doers: A Guide to Management Careers in the Nonprofit Sector.* New York: Foundation Center.

Coles, Robert. 1993. *Call to Service: A Witness to Idealism.* Boston: Houghton Mifflin.

Dove, K. E. 1988. *Conducting a Successful Capital Campaign.* San Francisco: Jossey-Bass.

Drucker, Peter. 1990. *Managing the Nonprofit Organization: Principles and Practice.* New York: Harper Collins.

Duronio, M. A., and E. R. Tempel. 1996. *Fundraisers: Their Careers, Stories, Concerns and Accomplishments.* San Francisco: Jossey-Bass.

Edles, L. P. 1993. *Fundraising: Hands-on Tactics for Nonprofit Groups.* New York: McGraw-Hill.

Edwards, Richard L., Elizabeth A. S. Benefield, Jeffrey A. Edwards, and John A. Yankey. 1997. *Building a Strong Foundation: Fundraising for Nonprofits.* Washington D.C.: National Association of Social Workers Press.

Galaskiewiz, Joseph, and Wolfgang Bielfeld. 1998. *Nonprofit Organizations in an Age of Uncertainty.* New York: Aldine De Gruyter.

Gies, David L. 1990. *The Nonprofit Organization: Essential Readings.* Pacific Grove, Calif.: Brooks/Cole Publishing.

Graham, C. 1992. *Keep the Money Coming: A Step by Step Strategic Guide to Annual Fundraising.* Sarasota, Fla.: Pineapple Press.

Hall, Peter Dobkin. 1992. *Inventing the Nonprofit Sector and Other Essays on Philanthropy, Volunteerism, and Nonprofit Organizations.* Baltimore: Johns Hopkins University Press.

Hopkins, Bruce. 1993. *The Law of Fund Raising.* New York: John Wiley and Sons.

Horton, C. 1991. *Raising Money and Having Fun (Sort Of): A "How To" Book for Small Non-Profit Groups.* Cleveland: May Dugan Center.

Howe, Fisher. 1991. *The Board Member's Guide to Fund Raising*. San Francisco: Jossey-Bass.

Mancuso, Anthony. *How to Form a Nonprofit Corporation in All Fifty States*. Berkeley, Ca.: Nolo Press.

Martin, Michael. 1994. *Philanthropy, Voluntary Service, and Caring*. Bloomington: Indiana University Press.

Montana, Patrick. 1978. *Marketing in Nonprofit Organizations*. New York: American Management Association.

Murray, Vic. 1991. *Improving Corporate Donations: New Strategies for Grantmakers and Grantseekers*. San Francisco: Jossey-Bass.

Neiheisel, Steven R. 1994. *Corporate Strategy and the Politics of Goodwill: A Political Analysis of Corporate Philanthropy in America*. New York: Peter Lang.

Prince, R. A., and K. M. File. 1994. *The Seven Faces of Philanthropy: A New Approach to Cultivating Major Donors*. San Francisco: Jossey-Bass.

Rosso, H. A. 1991. *Achieving Excellence in Fund Raising*. San Francisco: Jossey-Bass.

Rothman, Jack, Joseph Teresa, Terrence Kay, and Gershom Morningstar. 1983. *Marketing Human Service Innovations*. Beverly Hills, Calif.: Sage.

Selzer, Michael. 1987. *Securing Your Organization's Future: A Complete Guide to Fundraising Strategies*. New York: Foundation Center.

Shannon, James P. 1991. *The Corporate Contributions Handbook: Devoting Private Means to Public Needs*. San Francisco: Jossey-Bass.

Skloot, Edward. 1988. *The Nonprofit Entrepreneur: Creating Ventures to Earn Income*. New York: Foundation Center.

Powell, Walter W. 1987. *The Nonprofit Sector: A Research Handbook*. New Haven, Conn.: Yale University Press.

Rose-Ackerman, Susan. 1986. *The Economics of Nonprofit Organizations: Studies in Structure and Policy*. New York: Oxford University Press.

Schram, Barbara. 1997. *Creating Small-Scale Social Programs: Planning, Implementation, and Evaluation*. Thousand Oaks, Calif.: Sage.

Warrick, M. 1994. *How to Write Successful Fundraising Letters*. Berkeley, Calif.: Strathmoor Press.

Wolch, Jennifer. 1990. *The Shadow State: Government and Voluntary Sector in Transition*. New York: Foundation Center.

Notes

Chapter I

1. Race differences are significant, although most children live with their mothers. The incidence of single-parent households is lowest among whites (19.2 percent) and highest among African Americans (55 percent); among Hispanic families, the figure is 30 percent (U.S. Bureau of the Census 1990; compare Scanzoni 1995, 291–93).

2. Scanzoni 1995.

3. The average decline in standard of living for divorced mothers is 30 percent (Hoffman and Duncan 1988).

4. Abramowitz 1996.

5. Berrick (1995) for a fuller discussion of the rapid growth in the 1980s and early 1990s.

6. Reskin and Padavic 1994; U.S. Bureau of Labor Statistics 1995. There is significant variation by both age and race. For example, for white women, the gap narrows to about 80 percent of white males. For African American women, it widens to about 63 percent, and for Hispanic women, it widens even further to a dramatic 56 percent (U.S. Bureau of Labor Statistics 1995).

7. Rubin 1994, 121.

8. Wilson 1996.

9. Lorber 1994.

10. Clinton 1997; cf. Seccombe 1999, 37.

11. For example, Arkansas ranks forty-ninth of fifty-one (including the District of Columbia) in state poverty rates, with almost 20 percent of its population living below the poverty line, compared to the national average of about 13 percent (U.S. Census Bureau 1999a).

12. Chase-Landsdale and Brooks-Gunn 1995.

13. Swanson 1988.

14. Ibid.

135

Chapter 2

1. U.S. Bureau of Census 2000; Ferree and Hess 1994; Danzinger and Gottschalk 1995. Moreover, recent studies have shown that the absence of fathers does indeed have a negative psychological impact on children (McLanahan and Sandefur 1994).

2. Schram 1995, 175.

3. Seccombe 1999, 140.

4. Ibid., 224; Clark and Long 1995.

5. Phillips et al. 1994.

6. Phillips and Bridgman 1999; Adams and Sabelhaus 1995.

7. Abramowitz 1996.

8. Penny equates housing with the welfare system, but technically, low-income housing is provided by municipalities or by private companies whose buildings are publicly financed.

9. Today Laura would be able to keep a car of any value, assuming it was paid for, along with items up to $3,000 in worth. However, she would only be allowed to earn up to $223 per month in addition to her TEA assistance.

10. Edin and Lein 1997.

11. Bernstein, Brocht, and Spade-Aguilar 2000, 64. See also the Economic Policy Institute web page. Available: www.epinet.org.

12. Child care has been shown to be extremely problematic for many single parents, being of variable quality, often inadequate, and costly (Hayes, Palmer, and Zaslow 1990).

13. Abromowitz 1996; Bernstein 1993; Schram 1995; Seccombe 1999.

14. Rodman 1999.

15. The fifteen-hour work requirement has been flexibly interpreted, so that some recipients may count class or work-study time. The interpretation is essentially left up to the caseworker and is influenced by the county supervisor's attitude.

16. During the first two years that Act 1058 was in effect, the caseload of families receiving welfare dropped by over 43 percent.

17. U.S. Bureau of the Census 1995.

18. Litcher 1997.

19. Patterson 1994, 226.

20. U.S. Bureau of the Census 1998, "Poverty in the United States, Age, Race and Hispanic Origin." *Current Population Reports*, Series P-60-515. Washington D.C.: U.S. Printing Office. Available: http://www. census.gov/hhes/poverty98.

21. Thompson and Hickey 1999, 231.

Chapter 3

1. Dowd 1994; Feagin 1975.

2. Blendon et al. 1995; cf. Edin and Lein 1997.

3. Congressional Digest 1995; U.S. Committee on Ways and Means 1996.

4. Donahue 1994.

5. Huff 1996; Danziger and Gottschalk 1993; and Rosoff, Pontell, and Tillman 1998.

6. Greenberg 1993; Danziger and Lin 2000, 254; see U.S. Committee on Ways and Means 1996; see Bane and Ellwood 1986).

7. Seccombe 1999, 37.

8. Congressional Record 100th Congress 13 October 1988, H11418–11450.

9. Child Trends, Washington, D.C. (unpublished data from the 1991 National Survey of Children). Compare Chase-Landsdale and Brooks-Gunn 1995, 42.

10. Chase-Landsdale and Brooks-Gunn 1995, 42.

11. In the United States, the rate in 1979 was 16.2 percent, compared to 18.7 percent in 1998. See National Center for Children in Poverty, "Child Poverty in the States: Levels and Trends from 1979 to 1998" (New York: Columbia University's National Center for Children in Poverty). Available: http://cpmcnet.columbia.edu/dept/nccp.

12. It seems that Americans still have a difficult time believing that institutional racism is alive and well, and that it manifests itself in terms of educational opportunities and economic well-being. I find this especially true when it comes to discussions of affirmative action. An excellent analysis appears in Kozol 1991; see also Aronowitz and Giroux 1988.

13. Kerbo 1996, 270.

14. The "thrifty food plan" established as the "objective measure" for poverty was based on the assumption that food costs should not be

more than one-third of a household budget. For example, today a family of four with a pretax income of about $16,000 would be considered officially poor. But this measure is clearly outdated because while food costs have gone down as a proportion of average household budgets (some estimates are as low as one-sixth), many poor households spend up to 50 percent of their incomes on food alone. Also, a study by the Urban Institute revealed that 50 percent of families with incomes above 130 percent but below 200 percent of the poverty thresholds had worries about being able to buy food. These same families were not eligible for food stamps (eligibility is 130 percent above poverty guidelines). Finally, with the growing costs of housing and other living expenses, some analysts argue that a better estimate of the poor would include about 26 percent of the population. See Schwarz and Volgy 1992.

15. U.S. Bureau of the Census 1999a.

16. Guggliotta 1994.

17. Marger 1998, 225.

18. Seccombe 1999, 100.

19. Herrnstein and Murray 1984.

20. Goffman 1963.

21. Congressional Text—H.R. 1720, 13 October 1998.

22. Goffman 1963, 44–45; Seccombe 1999, 39.

23. G. H. Mead (1962) and C. H. Cooley (1902) wrote of the process by which we learn to evaluate ourselves. It is from the "generalized" other, Mead argues, that we form an evaluation of self, and thus come to imagine the worth of our contributions. Cooley described what he called the "looking glass" self, wherein we imagine how others view us and react according to this perception.

24. Smith and Stone 1989.

25. Ibid., 95.

26. U.S. Bureau of the Census 1999b.

27. Bernstein et al. 2000.

28. Echavarria, Restrepo, and Meza 1986; Halfon and Newacheck 1993; Starfield et al. 1991.

29. Neresian et al. 1985, Starfield 1991.

30. DiLeonardi 1993; Wolock and Horowitz 1984.

31. Cicerelli 1977; Leadbetter and Bishop 1994; McLeod and Shanahan 1993.

Chapter 4

1. Dr. Donna Darden posed this telling question in the first sociology course I took.

2. Banfield 1974.

3. Lewis 1966.

4. Rubin 1976, 211.

5. Swidler 1986. Swidler identifies a cultural "tool kit" (strategies of action that are determined by our social location) that often dictates the choices and decisions we make. If we have not been exposed to the idea of going to college or adhering to some middle-class value, rather than reject the notion we may simply deem it not plausible.

6. Waxman 1977, 43.

7. Bourdieu 1984.

8. Snow and Anderson 1987.

9. Mills 1959.

10. C. Everett Hughes (1945) was one of the first sociologists to discuss the important link between our occupations and our identities. While this was once true for men more than for women, that is changing drastically as women constitute an increasing share of the workforce and work assumes a more important place in their lives.

11. In fact, most of those who participated in the scholarship program have not only remained in Arkansas but have returned to their hometowns as productive citizens. Delta, for example, graduated with a 4.0 grade-point average and came back to her small town, first as a VISTA volunteer and later as director of the county affiliate for the Single Parent Scholarship Fund. Several of the women in this project now serve on their county's Single Parent Scholarship Fund board of directors.

12. Kerbo 1996, 333.

13. Hout 1988.

14. Baltzell 1958, Domhoff 1967, Kerbo 1996.

15. Featherman and Hauser 1978.

16. U.S. Bureau of the Census 1996.

17. Schultz 1994, Pirog and Magee 1997.

18. It is important to consider context as well. In the United States, women have greater opportunities for mobility than is true in other

countries, so that education can have greater impact. In China, for example, greater access to education and paid labor did not significantly increase empowerment for women (Wolf 1985).

19. Pinderhughes 1989, 56.

20. Sociologists interested in class relations under capitalism are more likely to see the college degree as a class divider. For example, as Robert Paul Wolff (1969) writes, "The real function of the Bachelor degree in our society is certification, all right, but it is class certification, not professional certification. The B.A. stamps a man as a candidate in good standing for the middle class. It is the great social divider that distinguishes the working class from the middle class" (p. 151).

21. Famightetti 1997; Marger 1999, 156.

22. Braun 1997, 22.

23. Bagby 1997.

24. In their book *Class Matters: Working-Class Women's Perspectives on Social Class* (1997), Pat Mahony and Christine Zmroczek bring together a group of essays on barriers that social class and gender create for women working in middle-class settings. One essay that I found especially interesting was "Switching Cultures," about the barriers present in academia and the consequences of crossing cultures. Bourdieu, Passerson, and Martin (1994) have much to say about the gate-keeping function of education as well.

25. Bowles and Gintis 1976.

26. Kozol 1991.

27. Good and Brophy 1973.

28. Jencks, Smith, and Acland 1972; Alexander, Cook, and McDill 1978.

29. Oakes 1985.

30. Featherman and Houser 1978, 309.

31. Jencks et al. 1979, 226.

32. Reskin 1998.

33. Even as early as 1959, Edgar Friedenberg was arguing that schools act as a sorting device to perpetuate an unequal society.

34. Criteria are often based on IQ scores, which are a highly controversial measure among sociologists and education researchers because of the connection between test scores and students' cultural, linguistic, and social capital (see Bourdieu 1977; Duster 1995; Hauser 1995;

and Weinstein 1997). Despite the fact that Herrnstein and Murray's book *The Bell Curve* has been criticized on many points, the notion that race has something to do with intellect has taken on a life all its own. See Oakes (1985) for a discussion of the implications and influence of race on educational achievement. Finally, see Coles (1987) for a critique of educational practices related to learning disabilities.

35. See also Neetles 1990, Steele 1992.

36. U.S. Bureau of the Census 1997a.

37. U.S. Bureau of the Census 1996.

38. U.S. Bureau of the Census 1997b.

39. O'Hare 1996.

40. U.S. Bureau of the Census 1997c.

41. Dye 1995, 185.

42. Sadker and Sadker 1994.

43. Fox 1989; Statham, Richardson, and Cook 1991.

44. Dye 1995.

45. Parsons 1942, 611.

46. Galinsky and Bond 1996.

47. Williams 1992.

48. Reskin and Padavic 1994, 32.

49. Dobrzynski 1996b. Brooks (1993) reported that women hold less than 6 percent of those occupations.

50. Bernstein 1996.

51. National Committee on Pay Equity 1995.

52. Reskin and Padavic 1994; Bielby and Bielby 1988; Cotter, DeFiore, and Hermsen 1997; Kanter 1977; Marsden, Kalleberg, and Cook 1993.

Chapter 5

1. Cross 1990.

2. U.S. Bureau of the Census 1997d.

3. Male high school graduates averaged $25,038 in annual earnings, compared to $53,560 for male college graduates (Thompson and Hickey 1999).

4. The process of social mobility can be painful, however. And the higher one's educational achievement, the harder the process may be.

Change is hardly automatic, and not everyone changes dramatically, but the subtle social cues of a middle-class surrounding do become familiar after a while. The results can be both positive and negative. In this study, many women noticed increased difficulty with family members, friends, and even intimate partners as they pursued their education. Those who were first-generation college students seemed to experience the most difficult adjustment.

    5. Lareau 1989.

    6. Hill and Stafford 1980; Lavin and Hyllegard 1996.

    7. Bourdieu 1977; DiMaggio and Mohr 1985.

Chapter 6

    1. Kaplan 1996.

    2. Because the program began as a grassroots organization, in its early days it depended heavily upon volunteer staff. This made it difficult to track the progress of graduates and drop-outs. Today the program conducts annual follow-up contacts with scholarship recipients from the previous year to help the Scholarship Fund improve its effectiveness.

    3. An in-depth look at the poverty thresholds and guidelines can be found on the University of Wisconsin's Institute for Research on Poverty website. Available: http://www.ssc.wisc.edu/irp.

    4. Information on incorporation can be obtained from the office of the Secretary of State.

    5. It is useful to obtain information on statutes which provide technical information and requirements for a particular state. This information may be free and available via the Secretary of State's office.

    6. The full text of the ASPSF constitution and by-laws can be found in Appendix A.

    7. Tocqueville 1966, 199.

    8. Neiheisel 1994, 78.

    9. I have provided a list of resources for those interested in forming their own nonprofit scholarship fund in Appendix B.

    10. Although the Arkansas Single Parent Scholarship Fund remains the only statewide program of its kind in the nation, other scholarship projects have been set up to benefit single parents in isolated areas throughout the United States. Unfortunately, they are still rare. One

program that has been especially innovative is at the University of Wisconsin–Madison. There not only are single parents able to apply for special scholarships, but a dorm has also been specifically designated for single parents. It was the dream of a professor of psychology, Nancy Denney, who was a single parent herself. After her death from breast cancer, a scholarship and the residence hall were established to help ease the burden for undergraduate students struggling with both academics and parenting. Other programs exist at state universities and community colleges across the country, but they remain small and underfunded.

Chapter 7

1. Center on Budget and Policy Priorities 1997. Located in Washington, D.C., the Center on Budget and Policy Priorities is a nonprofit organization that studies government spending and public policy issues that impact low- and moderate-income individuals.

2. Ibid., 23.

3. Ibid., 83.

4. Meyer and Cancian 1996.

5. Edin and Lein 1997, 140.

6. Stoesz 1997.

7. Edin and Lein 1997, xx.

8. Center on Budget and Policy Priorities 2000.

9. Ibid., vi.

10. Among those who have established state EITCs are Iowa, Maryland, Minnesota, New York, Rhode Island, Vermont, and Wisconsin.

11. Ibid., 122.

12. Center on Budget and Policy Priorities 1997, 126.

13. See the report "Working Families and the New Economy: How Are Arkansas Families Really Faring in Today's Job Market" (Good Faith Fund, Arkansas Advocates for Children and Families, and the Arkansas Public Policy Panel, Little Rock, Arkansas, October 2000). Available: http://www.arenterprise.org/public_policy.

14. Card 1992; Card and Krueger 1994. Two local studies conducted in Los Angeles and Baltimore confirmed these findings. See also the website for the Center for Community Change. Available: http://www.communitychange.org.

15. Center on Budget and Policy Priorities 1997, 14.

16. Siegel and Loman 1991; Seguino 1995.

17. Duran 2000, 4.

18. The Corporation for Enterprise Development is a national non-profit organization designed to assist poor families in establish credit and assets.

19. Edwards and Sherridan 1994.

20. Bowen and Bok 1999.

21. Lavin and Hyllegard 1996, 89.

22. Ibid., 91.

23. See the website for the Council on Adult and Experiential Learning. Available: http://www.cael.org.

Note: All web sites were verified to be accurate as of October 2001.

References

Abramowitz, Mimi. 1996. *Under Attack, Fighting Back: Women and Welfare in the United States*. New York: Monthly Review Press.

Adams, Gregory, and John Sabelhaus. 1995. "Trends in Out-of-Pocket Spending on Health Care, 1980–92." *Monthly Labor Review*, December.

Alexander, Karl, Martha Cook, and Edward McDill. 1978. "Curriculum Tracking and Educational Stratification: Some Further Evidence." *American Sociological Review* 43: 47-66.

Aronowitz, Stanley. 1990. "Between Nationality and Class." *Harvard Educational Review* 67, no. 2: 188–207.

Aronowitz, Stanley, and Henry Giroux. 1988. "Schooling, Culture and Literacy in the Age of Broken Dreams: A Review of Bloom and Hirsch." *Harvard Education Review* 58: 172–94.

Bagby, Merideth, ed. 1997. *Annual Report of the United States of America*. New York: McGraw-Hill.

Ballentine, Jeanne. 1997. *The Sociology of Education: A Systematic Analysis*. 4th ed. Englewood Cliffs, N.J.: Prentice-Hall.

Baltzell, Digby. 1958. *Philadelphia Gentlemen: The Making of a National Upper Class*. New York: Free Press.

Bane, M. J., and Ellwood, D. T. 1986. "Slipping into and out of Poverty: The Dynamics of Spells." *Journal of Human Resources* 21, no. 1: 1–23.

Banfield, Edwin. 1974. *The Unheavenly City Revisited*. Boston: Little, Brown.

Beeghley, Leonard. 1989. *The Structure of Social Stratification in the United States*. Needham Heights, Mass.: Allyn and Bacon.

Bernstein, Jared. 1993. "Rethinking Welfare Reform." *Dissent* (Summer): 277–79.

Bernstein, Jared, Chauna Brocht, and Maggie Spade-Aguilar. 2000. *How Much Is Enough? Basic Family Budgets for Working Families*. Washington, D.C.: Economic Policy Institute.

145

Bernstein, Nina. 1996. "Equal Opportunity Recedes for Most Female Lawyers." *New York Times,* January 8, A12.

Berrick, Jill Duerr. 1995. *Faces of Poverty: Portraits of Women and Children on Welfare.* New York: Oxford University Press.

Bielby, Denise D., and William T. Bielby. 1988. "She Works Hard for Her Money: Household Responsibilities and the Allocation of Work Effort." *American Journal of Sociology* 93: 1031-59.

Blendon, Robert J., Drew E. Altman, John Benson, Mollyann Brodie, Matt James, and Gerry Chervinsky. 1995. "The and the Welfare Reform Debate." *Archives of Pediatric and Adolescent Medicine* 149: 1065–69.

Bourdieu, Pierre. 1977. "Cultural Reproductions and Social Reproductions." In *Power and Ideology in Education,* ed. J. Karabel and A. H. Halsey, pp. 457–511. New York: Oxford University Press.

———. 1984. *Distinction: A Social Critique of the Judgement of Taste.* Cambridge, Mass.: Harvard University Press.

Bourdieu, Pierre, Jean-Claude Passerson, and Monique De Saint Martin. 1994. *Academic Discourse.* Stanford, Calif.: Stanford University Press.

Bowen, William G., and Derek K. Bok. 1999. *The Shape of the River: Long-Term Consequences of Considering Race in College and University Admissions.* Princeton, N.J.: Princeton University Press.

Bowles, Samuel, and Herbert Gintis. 1976. *Schooling in Capitalist America: Educational Reform and the Contradictions of Economic Life.* New York: Basic Books.

Braun, Denny. 1997. *The Rich Get Richer.* 2d ed. Chicago: Nelson-Hall.

Brooks, Nancy Rivera. 1993. "Gender Pay Gap Found Among Executives." *Los Angeles Times,* June 30, D1, D3.

Card, David. 1992. "Using Regional Variation in Wages to Measure the Effects of the Federal Minimum Wage." *Industrial and Labor Relations Review,* October.

Card, David, and Alan Krueger. 1994. "Minimum Wages and Employment: A Case Study of the Fast Food Industry in New Jersey and Pennsylvania." *American Economics Review* 84, no. 2 (September).

Center on Budget and Policy Priorities. Washington, D.C. www.cbpp.org

Chase-Landsdale, Lindsay P., and Brooks-Gunn, Jeanne, eds. 1995. *Escape from Poverty: What Makes a Difference for Children?* New York: Cambridge University Press.

Cicerelli, V.G. 1977. "Relationship of Socioeconomic Status and Ethnicity to Primary Grade Children's Self-Concept." *Psychology in the Schools* 14, no. 2: 213-15.

Clark, Ann L., and Andrew Long. 1995. *Child Care Prices: A Profile of Six Communities—Final Report.* Washington, D.C.: Urban Institute.

Clinton, Bill. 1997. "Welfare Should Be Reformed." In C. P. Cozic, ed., *Welfare: Opposing Viewpoints,* pp. 20-27. San Diego, Calif.: Greenhaven Press.

Coles, Gerald. 1987. *The Learning Mystique: A Critical Look at "Learning Disabilities."* New York: Pantheon.

Congressional Digest. 1995. Welfare Overview, June–July, pp. 163–165. Washington, D.C.: Government Printing Office.

Congressional Record. 1988. 100th Congress, 1st Session, H.R. 1720, 13 October (Z 1450 [CR(H11418–H11450)]).

Cooley, Charles Horton. 1902. *Human Nature and the Social Order.* New York: Schocken.

Cotter, David A., JoAnn DeFiore, and Joan M. Hermsen. 1997. "All Women Benefit: The Macro-Level Effect of Occupation Integration on Gender Earnings Equality." *American Sociological Review* 62 (October): 714–34.

Cross, Patricia K. 1990. *Adults as Learners.* San Francisco: Jossey-Bass.

Danziger, Shelton, and Peter Gottschalk. 1993. *Uneven Tides: Rising Inequality in America.* New York: Sage.

———. 1995. *America Unequal.* Cambridge, Mass.: Harvard University Press.

Danziger, Shelton, and Ann Chih Lin. 2000. *Coping with Poverty: The Social Contexts of Neighborhood, Work, and Family in the African-American Community.* Ann Arbor: University of Michigan Press.

DiLeonardi, J. W. 1993. "Families in Poverty and Chronic Neglect of Children." *Families in Society* 74, no. 9: 557–62.

DiMaggio, Paul, and John Mohr. 1985. "Cultural Capital, Educational Attainment, and Marital Selection." *American Journal of Sociology* 90: 1231–61.

Dobrzynski, Judith H. 1996a. "Study Finds Few Women in Five Highest Company Jobs." *New York Times,* October 18, C3.

———. 1996b. "Women Pass Milestone in the Board Room." *New York Times,* December 12, C4.

Domhoff, William. 1967. *Who Rules America?* Englewood Cliffs, N.J.: Prentice-Hall.

———. 1983. *Who Rules America Now? A View for the '80s.* Englewood Cliffs, N.J.: Prentice-Hall.

Donahue, James. 1994. *Aid for Dependent Corporations.* Washington, D.C.: Essential Information.

Dowd, Maureen. 1994. "Americans Like G.O.P. Agenda, But Split on How to Reach Goals." *New York Times,* December 15, A1.

Dubow, E. F., and M. F. Ippolilo. 1994. "Effects of Poverty and Quality of the Home Environment on Changes in the Academic and Behavioral Adjustment of Elementary School Age Children." *Journal of Clinical Child Psychology* 23, no. 4: 401-12.

Duran, Angela. 2000. "Self-Sufficiency: Assets as Critical as Income." In *Arkansas Working Families Project,* no. 2 (July). Available: http://www.arenterprise.org/public_policy/index.htm.

Duster, Troy. 1995. "Symposium: The Bell Curve." *Contemporary Sociology* 24, no. 2: 158–61.

Dye, Thomas V. 1995. *Who's Running America: The Clinton Years.* Englewood Cliffs, N.J.: Prentice Hall.

Echavarria, M. R., M. E. Restrepo, and E. M. Meza. 1986. "The Mother-Child Relationship in the Etiology of Severe Undernutrition." *Nutrition Reports International* 33, no. 3: 515–25.

Edin, Kathryn, and Laura Lein. 1997. *Making Ends Meet: How Single Mothers Survive Welfare and Low-Wage Work.* New York: Russell Sage Foundation.

Edwards, K., and M. Sherridan. 1994. *Individual Development Accounts.* Washington University, Saint Louis: Center for Social Development. http://gwbweb.wustl.edu/users/csd

Famightetti, Robert. 1997. *The World Almanac and Book of Facts.* New York: St. Martin's Press.

Feagin, Joe. 1975. *Subordinating the Poor: Welfare and American Beliefs.* Englewood Cliffs, N.J.: Prentice Hall.

Featherman, David, and Robert Hauser. 1978. *Opportunity and Change.* New York: Academic Press.

Fox, Mary Frank. 1989. "Women and Higher Education: Gender Differences in the Status of Students and Scholars." In *Women: A Feminist Perspective,* ed. Jo Freeman, pp. 217–35. Mountain View, Calif.: Mayfield Press.

Friedenberg, Edgar Z. 1959. *The Vanishing Adolescent.* New York: Dell.

Galinsky, Ellen, and James T. Bond. 1996. "Work and Family: The Experience of Mothers and Fathers in the U.S. Labor Force." In *The American Woman, 1996–1997,* ed. Cynthia Costello and Barbara Kivimae Krimgold, pp. 79–103. New York: W. W. Norton.

Gerdes, Karen. 1998. "Aid to Families with Dependent Children: Reform versus Reality." *Journal of Progressive Human Services* 9, no. 1: 45–62.

Goffman, Erving. 1963. *Stigma: Notes on the Management of Spoiled Identity.* Englewood Cliffs, N.J.: Prentice-Hall.

Good, T. L., and J. E. Brophy. 1973. *Looking in Class-Rooms.* New York: Harper and Row.

Gottschalk, Peter, and Sheldon Danziger. 1985. "A Framework for Evaluating the Effects of Economic Growth and Transfers on Poverty." *American Economic Review* 75, no. 1 (March): 153–61.

Greenberg, M. 1993. *Beyond Stereotypes: What State AFDC Studies on Length of Stay Tell Us about Welfare as a "Way of Life."* Washington, D.C.: Center for Law and Social Policy.

Griswold, Robert. L. 1993. *Fatherhood in America: A History.* New York: Basic Books.

Gugliotta, Guy. 1994. "The Minimum Wage Culture." *Washington Post National Weekly,* 3-9 October, 6.

Halfon, N., and P. Newacheck. 1993. "Childhood Asthma and Poverty: Differential Impacts and Utilization of Health Services." *Pediatrics* 91, no. 1: 56–61.

Hauser, Robert M. 1995. "Symposium: The Bell Curve." *Contemporary Sociology* 24, no. 2: 149–53.

Hayes, C. D., J. L. Palmer, and M. J. Zaslow, eds. 1990. *Who Cares for America's Children? Child Care Policy for the 1990s.* Washington D.C.: National Academy Press.

Herrnstein, Richard J., and Charles Murray. 1994. *The Bell Curve: Intelligence and Class Structure in American Life.* New York: Free Press.

Hess, Beth, and M. M. Ferree, eds. 1987. *Analyzing Gender: A Handbook of Social Science.* Newbury Park, Calif.: Sage.

Hill, R., and F. Stafford. 1980. "Parent Care of Children: Time Diary Estimates of Quantity, Predictability, and Variety." *Journal of Human Resources* 15: 219–39.

Hoffman, Saul D., and Greg Duncan. 1988. "What Are the Economic Consequences of Divorce?" *Demography* 25: 641–45.

Hout, Michael. 1988. "More Universalism, Less Structural Mobility: The American Occupation Structure in the 1980s." *American Journal of Sociology* 93: 1358–1400.

Huff, Daniel. 1995. "Upside-Down Welfare." In *Annual Editions: Sociology,* Kurt Finsterbusch ed., 24th edition, pp. 130–33. Guilford, Conn.: Dushkin.

Hughes, Everett. 1945. "Dilemmas and Contradictions of Status." *American Journal of Sociology* 50: 353–59.

Jencks, Christopher, Marshall Smith, and Henry Acland. 1972. *Inequality: A Reassessment of the Effect of Family and Schooling in America.* New York: Basic Books.

Kanter, Rosabeth Moss. 1977. *Men and Women of the Corporation.* New York: Basic Books.

Kaplan, A. E., ed. 1996. *Giving USA—1996.* New York: American Association of Fund Raising Counsel Trust for Philanthropy.

Kendall, Diana. 1999. *Sociology in Our Times.* 2d ed. Belmont, Calif.: Wadsworth.

Kerbo, Herold. 1996. *Social Stratification and Inequality.* 3d ed. New York: McGraw-Hill.

Kozol, Jonathan. 1991. *Savage Inequalities: Children in America's Schools.* New York: Crown.

Lareau, Annette. 1989. *Home Advantage: Social Class and Parental Intervention in Elementary Education.* Philadelphia: Falmer.

Lavin, David E., and David Hyllegard. 1996. *Changing the Odds: Open Admissions and the Life Chances of the Disadvantaged.* New Haven, Conn.: Yale University Press.

Leadbetter, B., and S. Bishop. 1994. "Predictors of Behavior Problems in Preschool Children of Inner-city Afro-American and Puerto Rican Adolescent Mothers." *Child Development* 65, no. 2: 638–48.

Lewis, Oscar. 1966. *La Vida: A Puerto Rican Family in the Culture of Poverty: San Juan and New York.* New York: Random House.

Litcher, Daniel T. 1997. "Poverty and Inequality among Children." *Annual Review of Sociology* 23: 121–70.

Lorber, Judith. 1994. *Paradoxes of Gender.* New Haven, Conn.: Yale University Press.

Luttrell, Wendy. 1997. *School-Smart and Mother-Wise: Working Class Women's Identity and Schooling.* New York: Routledge.

Mahony, Pat, and Cristine Zmroczek, eds. 1997. *Class Matters: Working Women's Perspectives on Social Class.* Bristol, Penn.: Taylor and Francis.

Marger, Martin, M. 1999. *Social Inequality: Patterns and Processes.* Mountain View, Calif.: Mayfield.

Marsden, Peter V., Arne L. Kalleberg, and Cynthia R. Cook. 1993. "Gender Differences in Organizational Commitment: Influences of Work Positions and Family Roles." *Work and Occupations* 20: 368–90.

McLanahan, S. S., and G. Sandefur. 1994. *Growing up with a Single Parent: What Hurts? What Helps?* Cambridge, Mass.: Harvard University Press.

McLeod, J., and M. J. Shanahan. 1993. "Poverty, Parenting, and Children's Mental Health." *American Sociological Review* 58: 351–66.

Mead, George Herbert. 1962. *Mind, Self, and Society.* Chicago: University of Chicago Press.

Meyer, Daniel, and Maria Cancian. 1996. "Life after Welfare: The Economic Well-Being of Women and Children Following an Exit from AFDC." Discussion Paper no. 1101-96. Madison: Institute for Research on Poverty, University of Wisconsin (August).

Mills, C. Wright. 1959. *The Sociological Imagination.* London: Oxford University Press.

Murray, Charles. 1984. *Losing Ground: American Social Policy 1950–1980.* New York: Basic Books.

National Committee on Pay Equity. 1995. "Wage Gap: Myths and Facts." In *Race, Class and Gender in the United States: An Integrated Approach,* ed. Paula S. Rothenberg, pp. 141–51. New York: St. Martin's Press.

Neetles, Michael. 1990. "Success in Doctoral Programs: Experiences of Minority and White Students." *American Journal of Education* 98 (August): 494–522.

Neiheisel, Steven R. 1994. *Corporate Strategy and the Politics of Goodwill: A Political Analysis of Corporate Philanthropy in America.* New York: Peter Lang.

Nerisian, W. S., M. R. Petit, R. Shaper, D. Lemieux, and E. Naor. 1985. "Childhood Death and Poverty: A Study of All Childhood Deaths in Maine 1976 to 1980." *Pediatrics* 75, no. 1: 41–50.

Oakes, Jeanne. 1985. *Keeping Track: How High Schools Structure Inequality.* New Haven, Conn.: Yale University Press.

O'Hare, William P. 1996. *A New Look at Poverty in America.* Washington, D.C.: Population Reference Bureau.

Parsons, Talcott. 1942. "Age and Sex in the Social Structure of the United States." *American Sociological Review* 7: 604–16.

Patterson, James. 1994. *America's Struggle against Poverty, 1990–1994.* Cambridge: Harvard University Press.

Phillips, Deborah, Miriam Voran, Ellen Kisker, and Carrollee Howes. 1994. "Child Care for Children in Poverty: Opportunity or Inequity?" *Child Development* 65, no. 2: 472–92.

Phillips, Deborah, and Anne Bridgman. 1999. "Frontiers of Research on Children, Youth, and Families." *Journal of Community Psychology* 27, no. 2: 511–16.

Pirog, Maureen, and Chris Magee. 1997. "High School Completion: The Influence of Schools, Families, and Adolescent Parenting." *Social Science Quarterly* 78: 710–24.

Pinderhughes, E.B. 1989. *Understanding Race, Ethnicity, and Power: The Key to Efficacy in Clinical Practice.* New York: Free Press.

Reskin, Barbara F. 1998. *The Realities of Affirmative Action in Employment.* Washington, D.C.: American Sociological Association.

Reskin, Barbara F., and Irene Padavic. 1994. *Women and Men at Work.* Thousand Oaks, Calif.: Pine Forge.

Rodman, Julie. 1999. "Medicaid and Welfare Reform." *Morning Edition,* National Public Radio, June 11.

Rosoff, Stephen, Henry Pontell, and Robert Tillman, 1998. *Profit Without Honor: White-Collar Crime and the Looting of America.* Upper Saddle River, N.J.: Prentice-Hall.

Rubin, Lillian B. 1976. *Worlds of Pain: Life in the Working-Class Family.* New York: Basic Books.

———. 1994. *Families on the Fault Line.* New York: Harper.

Sadker, Myra, and David Sadker. 1994. *Failing at Fairness: How America's Schools Cheat Girls.* New York: Scribner.

Scanzoni, John. 1995. *Contemporary Families and Relationships: Reinventing Responsibility.* New York: McGraw-Hill.

Schram, Sanford, F. 1995. *Words of Welfare: The Poverty of Social Sciences and the Social Science of Poverty.* Minneapolis: University of Minnesota Press.

Schultz, Fred, ed. 1994. *Annual Editions: Education, 1994/1995.* Guilford, Conn.: Dushkin.

Schwarz, John E., and Thomas J. Volgy. 1992. *The Forgotten Americans.* New York: W. W. Norton.

Seccombe, Karen. 1999. *"So You Think I Drive a Cadillac?" Welfare Recipients' Perspectives on the System and Its Reform.* Boston: Allyn and Bacon.

Seguino, Stephanie. 1995. *Living on the Edge: Women Working and Providing for Families in the Maine Economy, 1979–1993.* Margaret Chase Smith Center for Public Policy, University of Maine.

Siegel, Gary, and Anthony Loman. 1991. *Child Care and AFDC Recipients in Illinois: Patterns, Problems, and Needs.* Washington University, Saint Louis: Institute for Applied Research.

Smith, Kevin B., and Lorene H. Stone. 1989. "Rags, Riches, and Bootstraps: Beliefs about the Causes of Wealth and Poverty." *Sociological Quarterly* 30: 93–107.

Snow, David, and Leon Anderson. 1987. "Identity Work among the Homeless: The Verbal Construction and Avowal of Personal Identities." *American Journal of Sociology* 92, no. 6: 1336–71.

Starfield, B. 1991. "Childhood Morbidity: Comparisons, Clusters, and Trends." *Pediatrics* 88, no. 3: 519–26.

Starfield, B., S. Shapiro, J. Weiss, K. Liang, K. Ra, D. Paige, and X. B. Wang. 1991. "Race, Family Income, and Low Birth Weight." *American Journal of Epidemiology* 134, no. 10: 1167–74.

Statham, Anne, Laurel Richardson, and Judith Cook. 1991. *Gender and University Teaching: A Negotiated Difference.* Albany: State University of New York Press.

Steele, Claude M. 1992. "Race and Schooling of Black Americans." *Atlantic Monthly,* April, 268–78.

Stoesz, David. 1997. "Welfare Behaviorism." *Society,* March/April.

Swanson, Louis E. 1988. "The Human Dimensions of the Rural South in Crisis." In *The Rural South in Crisis,* ed. Lionel J. Beaulieu. Boulder, Colo.: Westview.

Swiddler, Anne. 1986. "Culture in Action: Symbols and Strategies." *American Sociological Review* 51: 273–86.

Thompson, William E., and Joseph V. Hickey. 1999. *Society in Focus.* 3d ed. New York: Addison Wesley Longman.

Tocqueville, Alexis de. [1835] 1966. *Democracy in America,* eds. J.P. Mayer and Max Lerner. New York: Harper Collins.

U.S. Bureau of the Census. 1995. "Poverty in the United States." *Current Population Reports.* Series P-60. Washington, D.C.: Government Printing Office.

———. 1996. "Educational Attainment in the United States: 1996." *Current Population Reports.* Series P-20-505. Washington, D.C.: Department of Commerce.

———. 1997a."Educational Attainment in the United States: March 1997." *Current Population Reports.* Series P-20-505. Washington, D.C.: Department of Commerce.

———. 1997b. "Median Net Worth by Race and Hispanic Origin of Householder and Monthly Household Income Quintile: 1993 and 1994." *Current Population Reports.* Series P-60. Washington, D.C.: Government Printing Office. Available: www.census.gov/hhes/www/wealth/1993wealth/93 html.

———. 1997c. Table 303: U.S. Department of Education, National Center for Educational Statistics, Degrees and Other Awards Conferred by Institutions of Higher Learning, 1960–2000. In *Statistical Abstract of the United States, 1997.* Washington, D.C.: Government Printing Office.

———. 1997d. "Age, Sex, Household Relationship, Race, and Hispanic Origin by Ratio of Income to Poverty Level, 1996." Washington, D.C.: Government Printing Office. Available: http://www.census.gov/prod/3/97pubs/, then select the link P60-199.PDF.

———. 1998a. "Money Income of Households, Families, and Persons in the United States: 1998." *Current Population Reports.* Series P-60, no. Washington, D.C.: Government Printing Office.

———. 1998b. "Poverty in the United States." *Current Population Reports.* Series P-60. Washington, D.C.: Government Printing Office. Available: http://www.census.gov/hhes/poverty/poverty98/pv98est1.html.

———. 1998c. *Statistical Abstract of the United States, 1998.* Washington, D.C.: Government Printing Office.

———. 1999a. Current Population Reports. In *Statistical Abstract of the United States, 1999,* pp. 20–513. Washington, D.C.: Government Printing Office.

———. 1999b. Current Population Reports. In *Statistical Abstract of the United States, 1999.* Series P60-206. Washington, D.C.: Government Printing Office.

———. 2000. *Overview of Entitlement Programs* (Greenbook). Washington, D.C.: Government Printing Office.

U.S. Bureau of Labor Statistics. 1995. Employment and Earnings (January). Washington, D.C.: U.S. Department of Labor.

U.S. House of Representatives, Committee on Ways and Means. 1996. *1996 Green Book.* Washington, D.C.: U.S. Government Printing Office.

Waxman, Chaim I. 1977. *The Stigma of Poverty: A Critique of Poverty Theories and Policies.* New York: Pergamon.

Weinstein, Michael. 1997. "The Bell Curve Revisited by Scholars." *New York Times,* October 11, A20.

Williams, Christine. 1992. "The Glass Escalator: Hidden Advantages for Men in the Female Professions." *Social Problems* 39: 253–67.

Wilson, William Julius. 1996. *When Work Disappears: The World of the New Urban Poor.* New York: Alfred A. Knopf.

Wolf, Margery. 1985. *Revolution Postponed: Women in Contemporary China.* Stanford, Calif.: Stanford University Press.

Wolff, Robert Paul. 1969. *The Ideal of the University.* Boston, Mass: Beacon Press.

Wolock, I., and B. Horowitz. 1984. "Child Maltreatment as a Social Problem: The Neglect of Neglect." *American Journal of Orthopsychiatry* 54, no. 4: 530–43.

Note: All web sites were verified to be accurate as of October 2001.

Index

157